With the sheer mass and number of UFO contacts happening all over the world today, a book produced just for abductees was bound to emerge. Michelle LaVigne has courageously taken the task to heart and has written her own remedial survival guide to ease one through the darkest hours of trial, regain lost power and restore one's sanity from the fiery baptism and complex aftermath of a UFO experience.

Abductees need to know, for they are often involved in an inner and outer conflict. They are faced with trauma, turmoil and criticism that evolves around the strange, wondrous UFO initiation. An alien encounter has the ability to carry away the strongest of souls in a whirlwind storm of emotional upheaval that shatters the presence of established reality. Without anchored faith or human support, all hopes and dreams of normalcy are smashed against the towering wall of darkness and fear. An abductee knows very well the feelings of rejection and abandonment and suffers in silence, and because of this, only a tip of the iceberg is exposed. Many wear masks to hide themselves from a critical, self-righteous world—a world that lacks mercy and love towards those claiming to have had UFO encounters. No wonder abductees suffer from dissociative personalities. Society's collective consciousness remains locked in denial of extraterrestrial visitation and phenomenon, making the needed integration process of the Gemini (twin) worlds appear to be impossible for the experience.

Daring to glance past subconscious shadows, into truth and light within, will break the chains and cycle of doubt that bar the door to freedom. Having seen tomorrow, abductees must survive for the future good. Today there is hope. Michelle's ideas allow the abductee to put their experience into perspective, to realize they are not alone, that others walk with them in this secret community or extraterrestrial world. *The Alien Abduction Survival Guide* may be an aid to help one through the journey and psychological maze created by a UFO experience. I heartily recommend reading this book.

Betty Andreasson Luca
lifetime ET experiencer

The Alien Abduction Survival Guide

How to Cope with Your ET Experience

by Michelle LaVigne

Wild Flower Press
P. O. Box 726
Newberg, OR

Library of Congress Cataloging-in-Publication Data
Michelle LaVigne. 1962-
The alien abduction survival guide: how to cope with your ET experience / Michelle LaVigne.

p. cm.

TL789.L338 1995
133.9---dc20   95-5644
                           CIP

ISBN 0-926524-27-5: $11.95
1. Unidentified flying objects--Sightings and encounters--Psychological aspects. 2. Abduction--Psychological aspects. 3. Victims--Mental health. I. Title.

DESIGN IMPLEMENTATION: Carlene Lynch
COVER DESIGN: Marcia Barrentine

Printed in the United States of America

Address all inquiries:
Wild Flower Press
P. O. Box 726
Newberg, OR 97132
U.S.A.

Printed on recycled paper.

Table of Contents

Michelle LaVigne

Michelle is in her early thirties and is a mother of three children. She worked as an Electro-Mechanical CAD Designer for various computer companies for many years before dedicating herself fully to writing about her ET encounters.

She comes from a family that has had a long history of abduction by the little gray ETs. Some of her relatives, as well as her youngest daughter, are all involved.

She has had hypnotic regression from Harvard psychiatrist, John Mack, who wrote the 1994 book, *Abduction*. Although she had hypnotic regression, she has had a relatively complete conscious memory of what has happened to her over the past sixteen years.

Michelle now spends her time with her family, as well as working with support groups on the Internet and writing magazine articles about ET encounters.

Foreword

On Memorial Day weekend, 1995, a prestigious international conference titled "When Cosmic Cultures Meet" was held in Washington D.C. The purpose of the conference was to bring world leaders in science, religion, government, military science, journalism and other fields together to discuss what the world's response should be when it is revealed to the public that we are in touch with beings from elsewhere.

Among the eminent guests was Dr. John E. Mack, M.D., Professor of Psychiatry at Harvard Medical School's Cambridge Hospital, Founding Director of the Center of Psychology and Social Change, and winner of a Pulitzer Prize. Included in his comments was a statement that he was willing to wager his 40 years of professional psychiatric practice that the alien abduction phenomenon is not simply a psychological aberration.

Dr. Mack has, indeed, wagered his career—literally. His success in bringing alien abductions to the public's attention with his bestselling book, *Abduction,* triggered an investigation that threatened his academic standing. He threw all the weight of his considerable credentials behind a wake-up slap in the face of humanity, and it landed squarely on Harvard University's unamused cheek. Like many other institutions (and like thousands of individuals) before it, Harvard is attempting to preserve its image of calm conservatism by distancing itself from what it considers a "fringe" subject.

Apparently, Harvard has not yet realized what thousands of abductees were forced to accept some years ago, and what such excellent researchers as Raymond Fowler, Budd Hopkins, David Jacobs, Leonard Stringfield, Linda Moulton Howe, Leah Haley, Karla Turner, John Carpenter, Robert Dean and a host of others have documented: Alien abduction is not a fringe subject. Alien abductions are very real.

Harvard's position is very understandable. It is based on fear. Fear of ridicule, the loss of funds, the loss of prestige, the soiling of an excellent reputation. And it is symptomatic of the worldwide attitude of denial that must be overcome before humanity can come to terms with the abduction phenomenon.

I researched abductions for many years prior to writing *Visitors From Time*. I knew some of them were real. But it was not until I began receiving invitations to speak at UFO conferences across the country that my eyes were opened to the astonishing magnitude of the phenomenon. It involves at least thousands of people in the United States alone (perhaps as many as five million, according to a survey conducted by the Roper Organization in 1991). And it appears to be only one aspect of a massive, ancient, systematic program of contact, spiritual conditioning, genetic manipulation and social engineering that is being carried out on Earth by several types of intelligent beings from somewhere else.

The evidence for this is clear and abundant, and freely available for anyone who wishes to pursue it. But the majority of the population does not pursue it because they are in a classic state of denial. People are simply unwilling to admit that Homo Sapiens may not be the pinnacle of God's Creation (or of evolution). They are unwilling to consider that other intelligences—perhaps millions of them—may have been created (or may have evolved or even been seeded) on other planets or in other dimensions, and that some of them may be far more intelligent and more technologically advanced than we. They are so unwilling to contend with the economic, religious, social and personal implications of contact with such beings that they simply refuse to accept it. And people are so frightened to think that these entities have the ability to pass through their walls in the middle of the night, anesthetize them, take them aboard their craft and perform invasive medical procedures on them that they trick themselves into believing that such things could not happen.

Because of this extraordinary human capacity for denial—and also because many psychotherapists fear the same sorts of problems feared by Harvard—thousands of abductees are left to learn how to cope with their reality-shattering experiences virtually on their own. Many have sought professional help, only to be disillusioned because their therapists did not believe in alien abductions, and therefore tried to diagnose them with, and treat them for, ailments they did not have. This practice has made their condition worse, rather than better. Others have located one of the very few psychotherapists who are well-versed in the subject, but many abductees have been unable to pay for professional services, or have had to go to the back of a long line of abductees equally in need of help. Still others, despairing at the lack of professional help, have asked untrained amateur UFO investigators to hypnotize them, and have come away more confused than they were to begin with.

As a consequence of this state of affairs, we ufologists often find ourselves acting as part-time, ad hoc, pro bono counselors. Abductees often seek us out and say, "I think I'm an abductee, and I'm thinking about hypnosis; what should I do?" It happens every day. And what should we do? We are not qualified to counsel them.

The best we can do is ask them a few questions to determine whether or not they fit known patterns for abductees. If they do, we can try to find psychotherapists who understand abduction phenomena (a nearly impossible task in most areas) and hope they do not charge for their services, or that the abductees can afford them (since insurance companies do not recognize alien abduction syndrome as a "covered illness"). If they do not fit known patterns, we can recommend they find "regular" psychotherapists and hope that they are treated well. And meanwhile we can listen to their stories with compassion and without judgment, reassure them that they are certainly not alone, and try to find support groups—or at least discussion groups—for them.

But all this is pitifully inadequate. It is not working. Thousands of people all over the world are forced to deal with experiences even more frightening and mind-shattering than being raped, and they have virtually no coping skills.

That is why this book is so important.

The Alien Abduction Survival Guide does not try to prove anything. It is not an edict handed down from some ivory tower. It is written by an abductee for abductees. The author, Michelle LaVigne, is not a UFO investigator. She is neither a professional writer, nor a psychiatrist. She is a former design engineer and a mother of three. Her family has been subjected to generations of abductions by diminutive gray beings. She has conscious memories of these encounters throughout her life, dating back to infancy.

Michelle makes no attempt to use landing-site photographs, footnoted quotes and correlations from other books to convince anyone that abductions are real. She knows that the people who need this book already *know* abductions are real because they have been living with them. She simply shares the information she has learned and the coping skills she has developed during a lifetime of learning to deal with her own abduction experiences.

Her words are informal, unpretentious and genuine, her approach straightforward and easy to understand. She offers practical tips for abductees on how to identify patterns of fear, how to lessen stress for loved ones, how to find professional help and other important topics. She reassures abductees, not only by her own example (she has always been brought back safely), but also by explaining to them the minute details of how the abduction process works. (After all, fear of the unknown is the most powerful of all fears, and knowledge is indeed power over it.)

Michelle even includes a glossary of terms, a list of resources, an essential reading list, and an appendix written specifically to help abductees' support people learn to cope with the situation from their perspectives. She presents methods by which an abductee can overcome fear, assimilate what is happening and graduate beyond fear and into growth. These techniques are not esoteric, expensive or elusive. They are pragmatic, and they work, regardless of one's preconceptions and despite one's individual experiences.

For a few more weeks or months, perhaps even for a few years, we can continue to close our eyes to the fact that alien abductions are occurring, but ignoring the abductions will not make them go away. We all will need to learn how to deal with them, and this book can help us do that.

Marc Davenport
author of *Visitors From Time*
June 15, 1995

Introduction

This guide book is very different from other books you may have read about abduction phenomena. It's not a collection of scary stories whose purpose is to convince you that abduction events are real. It is not a book channeled by some unseen force who claims to know everything about aliens (or even to be one). It's a guide written by an experienced alien abductee to help other abductees deal with the exceedingly unusual events of their lives. It's a guide to coping with—and maybe even thriving in—the perplexing world of alien abduction phenomena. It is a practical look at problems faced by abduction experiencers, and includes some solutions to these problems that have been tried and really work.

Often, we abductees are told that nothing can help. But that's not really true. *The Alien Abduction Survival Guide* will help you confront feelings and fears associated with the alien abduction experience, and offer you ways to take back control of your life.

As you probably know all too well, alien abduction is not a thing of fantasy. It's really happening to countless thousands of people all over the world. People just like you. Some understand—or at least accept—what's happening to them. Many more, however, are confused and afraid.

Since knowledge is the key to understanding, knowing what could be happening to you is the first step to knowing who you truly are and what you can do about your situation.

You see, you're not just like everyone around you. Your life experiences are coming from two very different places. Both are equally real to you and both affect all you are, despite how much you remember about the world I've come to call the "Secret Community."

This Secret Community is a place unlike anything bound to Earth. It's a world of strange visions and sounds. It's a world of blue light, red diamonds and swirling spheres of color. It's a place where the people are not from our world, at least the world we know in our everyday lives. And since you've seen this place, you are a part of the Secret Community.

We, the people involved in this unusual way of life, are quite different from the people around us. Experiencers are an extraordinary group of bright, intelligent, well-adjusted individuals. ("Experiencer" is the term most of the people I know prefer to be called. I will use "experiencer" and "abductee" in this book as if they were the same word, giving neither word more meaning than the other.) We tend to have highly skilled (though not always recognized) psychic senses, and keen abilities to feel and reflect the emotions of others.

On the other hand, we also seem to find it difficult to feel part of a group. Often we tend to feel out of place even around people whom we know well. Our experiences make us different from the others around us, and we usually seek out alternatives to the common belief systems in place around us.

Often, abductees do not settle for easy answers. We want to know the whys behind everything, and we aren't satisfied with cop-out answers like "just because."

These tendencies may have caused you problems with your relationships. Many abductees find it hard to be satisfied with an imperfect relationship. They dream that an ideal mate is out there somewhere. Many times this is because the experiencer does have strong, loving relationships in the Secret Community.

Experiencers may also find themselves at contention with their religion. Many times they search from one faith to another, hoping to find answers to questions they cannot even begin to put into words.

Unfortunately, for most abductees, there really isn't a set place to find useful information about what they are going through. And, whether they have just discovered they are an experiencer or have known it all their lives, they're full of questions about themselves and what's happening to them in this secret world.

When I started looking to others for help in understanding my abductions, I found that I had more conscious memory than many of my colleagues. My mentor, Hetar, told me that this is because I am to teach others living in this world about their place in the Secret Community. The best way to do this is by showing them ways they can help themselves to understand the details of their particular experiences.

With that in mind, let me tell you a little about me and my place in this Secret Community, so that you can understand why I know how you feel and can offer you some help.[1]

1. As you read, keep in mind that this book is not gender specific. In some chapters I refer to "she" and in others I use "he," but this is only for ease of reading. Except for the sections dealing with fetuses, etc., all of the topics I discuss apply equally to both males and females.

chapter one

My Beginnings

My name is Michelle and I am in my early thirties. I have three children, and until my youngest daughter came along, I worked as an electromechanical CAD designer. (I used computers to design instruments for various companies.) I went to technical college and was on the dean's list.

I grew up in Massachusetts. I was the third of four children in a family of French-Canadians (with some Canadian Indian thrown in for good measure). My family has a long history of abduction by the little gray aliens. My experiences have led to believe that many of my relatives, as well as my youngest daughter, are involved. My daughter is the only one who will talk about it.

Aside from writing this book, I have worked with other experiencers who have set up a network of support that will nurture its members rather than study them. I'm also in touch with PEER (Program for Extraordinary Experience Research). (See appendix three.)

So far I've undergone only one hypnotic regression. It was conducted by Dr. John E. Mack, M.D., of Harvard University, a renowned expert in the abduction field. The session was a great help in getting me over a block in my memory. I had a relatively complete conscious memory of most of what had happened to me during the previous sixteen or more years, but for some reason I couldn't bring myself to face a certain event. The session helped me deal with it and move on. (Though hypnosis is a very useful tool, sometimes it's just not necessary and can complicate things. The possible advantages and disadvantages of hypnosis should be considered carefully for each event.)

My very first memories of contact involve a tall, pale, very thin man I call Hetar. (See Figure 1.) He is my mentor. You may know him; you may not. But I'm sure you know someone like him. Many experiencers perceive these mentors as "the chief doctor" or even their "handlers."

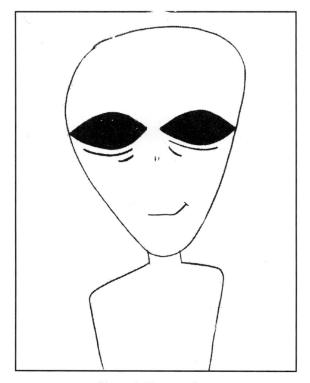

Figure 1. Hetar smiling.

My earliest memories are a bit vague. I remember lying in my crib when I was so small that I could barely lift my head. I opened my eyes and looked through the yellow crib rails. On the other side of the bars was a small being with ashen gray skin and large, black, almond-shaped eyes. He smiled at me and talked softly. I heard his thoughts and could understand what he was saying.

He said, "Be a good girl. Be strong and make me proud."

I don't remember if I replied. I don't think I could.

Another memory I have of the gray people is rather scary to think about, and to the average person could sound very strange. But to you—a fellow experiencer—it may sound familiar.

I remember lying on a table in a brightly lit, white room with curving walls. I saw a large control board on the wall, and a black table with shining silver devices and instruments on it. Along the top of the room was a catwalk with a black railing. I couldn't move. Hetar stood at my left, just inside my peripheral vision. Several smaller greys were working on my body. They seemed to be getting ready for something special. I started to get a little concerned and asked, "What are you doing?"

Hetar replied in his frank, but sometimes unappreciated, honesty, "We're going to take your lungs out. Does that scare you?" His tone was matter-of-fact, as if it really shouldn't bother me—but it did.

I have undergone these kinds of strange medical abductions throughout my life on a regular basis. But I'm sure that's no surprise to you. After all, like me, you're a member of this Secret Community, living two totally different, distinct lives and trying to cope with a world of human values and deal with a soul-shaking experience that most people around you won't even believe. Whether you believe this is a good or bad thing, whether you feel the victim or the blessed, you have an awesome paradox in front of you. You have to assimilate both phases of yourself into one whole person and grow. You have to learn to deal with the pain and fear, and go on. You have to find your space in life. But I have no doubt that you will.

Since I have been exploring my inner self and helping others around me discover theirs, I have seen many spread out their wings and fly. To understand what makes us what we are is to take control. And to be in control is all most people really want from life anyway...isn't it?

I hope this book will help give you that control. My purpose here is to share what I have experienced. I don't claim to have all the answers, but hopefully what I have learned will help make your life easier.

chapter two

Levels of Experience

There are many levels of abduction experiences. I feel it's important for you to understand the major levels and where you may fit into it all so that you can begin to understand what's happening to you. Then you can begin to take control of your life.

If you recognize yourself or your experiences as you read on, please realize that these levels are not always going to be your lot in life. Many people grow and progress through levels, while some are born to do certain jobs. Some even digress back through these stages (but this is rare).

One-Time Incidents

The first level is what I call one-time incidents. This level includes people who are picked up for a specific reason and are (usually) never bothered again.

For example, let's say a man who lives on your street has been an experiencer all his life. He's also an active member in the alien breeding project. One night the ETs pick this man up and give him a physical examination before they draw his genetic material from him. During this examination, they find that he has an unusually high level of lead in his blood. They become concerned and curious about where the lead is coming from. They return to the street where this man lives and pick up a few people from the area who are not regular subjects to check the levels of lead in their blood. If they don't find what they are looking for, they might even pick up others involved with this man, such as co-workers and friends. If you happen to be one such person, you may be picked up.

The one-time incident may or may not remember anything has happened to her and will likely never be picked up again.

I have found that these people seldom seek out help. I presume that is because their memories of their encounters (if they have any memories) are too vague or too strange to believe. So they assume their encounters are bad dreams and forget them. With no further intervention from the ETs, they may never have occasion to think about it again.

Quick in/Quick outs

Another level of abduction is what I call the "drive-through method." The Gemini people (another level of experiencers I describe next) call subjects of these abductions "quick in/quick outs." It appears to me that the vast majority of abductions are of this type. Quick in/quick out experiences usually follow this pattern:

The people are collected—often from their beds—and are taken onto a ship, where they are unable to move or control their actions. Small gray ETs lead them to a waiting area. Sometimes (but not always) the greys undress them. Then they lead them into examination rooms.

Sometimes they must stand in a long line of quick in/quick outs along a long curved hallway. If they are placed in this line, they will be led into a very large room with many tables where a lot of quick in/quick outs are having procedures done in a production-line fashion.

When the procedures they were abducted for are finished, they are returned home. The whole abduction may take only a few hours or less. The people usually awake at home having no idea of what has just transpired. Sometimes they have some bleeding in their ears or noses, or may have cuts or red marks they notice before they fall asleep for the balance of the night. These marks are almost always gone by the time they awaken for the day. Once in a while, a thin white scar may be left behind.

In general, quick in/quick out experiencers are unable to move independently and seldom say more than a mumble or a cry when with the ETs. Many of them tell me that the inability to move is often more frightening than the abduction itself.

Gemini People

The name "Gemini" was chosen by the people of the Secret Community. It was chosen not because of astrological signs, but because it is symbolic of the double life we lead. (Actually, I'm a Pisces.)

I have found that the Gemini people tend to be the most inquisitive about what's happening to them. Based on my experience with other abductees, I can say with a good degree of confidence that, if you are reading this to discover more about yourself and the unusual life you lead, then you are probably in this category of abduction experience. You are seeking your place in the Community.

The people involved in this level of experience are more likely to be picked up more frequently than the average quick in/quick outs. Though many people from this level started among the ranks of the quick in/quick outs, others have been in this category from birth.

Gemini people are the main building blocks of the ET-built Community. They have more control over what happens during abduction events and can have very strong social bonds to ETs and/or other experiencers they interact with while with the ETs.

As working members of this Community, they may still be involved with physical aspects of the experiences, but are also being exposed to spiritual sides of the events. Often Gemini experiencers are invited to talk with ETs. Most even attend classes taught by other, more skilled Geminis or ETs. This "classroom" aspect—like other positive aspects of abduction events—is seldom (if ever) discussed in the media, possibly because it does not generate high ratings as do the scary, "they-are-out-to-get-you" stories.

This is one reason why Geminis are confused when they begin to explore their experiences on a conscious level. They constantly experience the bittersweet situation of having a loving sense of community and the joy of the lessons, tempered always with the fear of the procedures and the pain of the perceptions/reaction test. Throw in a few hours of films filled with terrified people and skeptics, and it's a bag of mixed messages. This is especially true if they only remember the physical side of their experiences, because the spiritual side is always there inside, saying, "You need this."

Partial memory and mixed messages can really confuse a person. I remember an event during which I was being subjected to a terrible numbing pain. I couldn't breathe, and every nerve in my body was dancing with electric charge. I just couldn't stand the pain anymore and broke away.

Hetar, who was standing at my side, said, "You have been a bad girl. I'll have to take you home now." And he did.

I woke up so confused. I was really upset that he took me home, but I couldn't understand why. At that point in my personal discovery, I believed I would have given my right arm if they would just take me home. After all, everything and everyone around me was telling me I was a victim.

The confusion I was feeling followed me for days. It wasn't until much later—when I began to believe in my own memories and not what the media were telling me—that I discovered that the physical side is not the only side to the experience. As it turned out, I was upset about going home because I missed out on taking part in, and interacting with, the rest of the Community.

As in any structured society, everyone in the Gemini community has a job to do. Just about everyone is a community worker in some way or another. Workers are the people who are trained (often from a very early age) to do a specific job or jobs for the ETs. If you fall into this category, you may be a Teacher, Controller, Child-care giver or Empath, to name a few. Every one of these jobs is very specific and specialized. If you do one of these jobs, it will be a very big part of you. You will feel a burning need to do your job—you have to. Your job is an inseparable part of who and what you are.

Teachers

If you are a teacher, you may work with groups of humans, halflings or both. (Halflings are hybrids that are part human, part ET. Although the name implies they are half human, that's not always the case.) You may work with children, teens or even adults. Often, teachers work with several different ages in several different groups. The subjects taught can range from understanding Earth changes to coping with your dual lives. Many times people remember teaching others how to identify and use strange alien objects and tools. Often they can remember seeing the tools, but don't remember what they were or what was said about them.

Although classes usually take place in rooms that look very much like the rest of the ship (with curving, white walls, rounded doorways, etc.), I have taught classes in rooms that looked like old high schools. They are created to look like that on purpose. You walk down a curving, smooth, white corridor and through a door on the left to find yourself in what appears to be the hall of a high school.

Often the students learning things here are adults. They usually think they are dreaming about being back in school. Even though they are taught subjects not usually addressed in Earth schools (such as universal order, nonlinear time structure and the like), they usually believe they are simply having a really strange dream. If you have dreamed of being in a strange school with hallways that seemed to go on forever, yet not go anywhere, you are probably a student or teacher in what I have come to call UFO High.

Some teachers work one-on-one with gifted individuals. One-on-one contact is very important, particularly when training a person to work in the higher levels of teaching. The ETs don't take the training of their teachers lightly. Even though, in the purest sense of the word, we are all teachers of humankind, if you teach other Geminis, you worked hard to earn that honor. Learning to be a teacher can be a very personal, very intimate journey. It's not something anyone should have to do in a group.

Let me give you an example, and you'll see what I mean. In one of my capacities as a teacher, I train others to be teachers. One of the first things a new worker must do before she is allowed to teach is to confront her inner faults and weaknesses. It's difficult, but it's necessary for the growing process.

In order to teach this, I use a series of small, dark gray, metallic balls. They were about the size of croquet balls. The balls sit in a rack of four shelves, one ball on each shelf. Each ball, from the top down, raises the intensity of the vision revealed to its holder. For example, the top ball may make you see yourself as others see you, but with your major personality flaws accentuated a bit. By the time you get to the last ball, you are seeing all the embarrassments and regrets you have ever had, as well as every imperfection in your soul.

These things are exceedingly dramatic and completely soul-shaking. But when you are aware of the worst in you, you are much more able to unconditionally accept others with all their dark imperfections. The purpose is to never let you forget that, no matter what position you hold over others, you are just the same, just as imperfect, as anyone else—maybe even more, if you let your ego get so out of hand. And believe me, nothing can put you back in perspective faster and more effectively than a slap of your own ego across your face.

An even more important purpose of these tools is to allow you to face things about yourself that you don't like, but cannot change. After you begin to face these things, you can begin to accept yourself as you are—despite what you might think is wrong with yourself.

Using these balls is not as easy as it sounds. Let me illustrate.

I was working with a woman in her late twenties. She had just progressed up from some other task she did well, and Hetar felt she was ready to learn to teach. Of course, she felt she could take on the world.

She had a pretty good psychic sense (for which she used to get a lot of attention from her Earthbound associates, I was told). Her ego was massive; she truly felt she was "the chosen one." (Actually her attitude is not uncommon. Many people go through a period of feeling like the "chosen one" to protect themselves from facing their total experience.)

Hetar brought her to me. I was in the discovery room (as I like to call it), a long, dimly lit room with one rack of four balls on the side of the room where I was standing. About thirty paces away, on the other side of the room, was another identical rack, but it was empty.

I greeted the woman and Hetar. He told me she felt ready. He said she had been working really hard and believed it was time to move up. I asked if she really was ready.

He nodded to me and turned to her. "Listen carefully, and be a good girl," he told her. "This job is very important." Then he walked out of the room.

I turned to watch him leave. I waited until he was gone and the door was closed before I turned to the girl. She was standing with her hand on her hip, tapping her foot on the floor.

"OK, so what's my new job?" she asked.

I picked up the first ball. "Do you see this?" I put it back onto the rack. "You have to pick it up and carry it to that rack over there and put it in the top holder."

She got really aggravated. "Oh, I can't believe this bull," she complained. "What kind of stupid job is this? I worked so damned hard for this? You can't believe all I went through to get this damn job!"

The whole time she raved, I stood quiet and unmoving. After she was through, I picked up the ball one more time. "From here to there," I said. "And it's not as easy as it looks." I put the ball down.

With a final, very expressive sigh, she picked up the ball and began to walk across the room. (See Figure 2.) I watched her eyes as she seemed to stare far into the distance. Her steps slowed, then stopped after only three or four paces. She dropped the ball and fell to the floor in tears. Right away, two small greys came in and led her away. I picked up the ball and put it away, thinking, "She did pretty well, considering...."

Figure 2. A woman learning a lesson in the discovery room.

The next time we had a session with the gray balls in the discovery room, she was a much more receptive student, ready to really learn something about who she is.

You can see how important "private lessons" are. If the woman were to experience this type of thing in a group setting, she would be compelled to feel shame in front of the others who saw it happen. That would not be productive. She did nothing wrong—at least nothing you or I aren't capable of doing, too. So we can't judge her.

Child-Care Givers

Although every Gemini is always around children (all kinds of children, both human and halfling), some Gemini experiencers have the specific duty of watching these children, playing games with them, telling them stories or simply holding them and giving them love. These child-care givers are chosen because they have an incredible maternal or paternal instinct and so are able to shower lots of love on these children.

This job is different from the bonding events that everyone seems to go through at one time or another. Those events, during which a person is asked to hold or love a baby, are common among all abductees. Child-care givers don't just hold one baby, once in a while. They are surrounded by children most of the time. They are the keepers of the nursery, the den mothers and troop leaders. They are the nannies and parents to everyone else.

Like teachers, child-care givers must work hard to achieve their positions. They have to learn to love all the children in their care, no matter what race, color or species they are. And they do.

Controllers

Another job a Gemini may have is that of the controller. This job is difficult to explain. There are different levels of controller, and as the levels get more involved and cross over into the work of the empaths (see next section), you find that the tasks given men and women start to differ. For example, in the lower levels, both men and women are controllers. They move among the quick in/quick outs in the waiting areas, talking to them in soothing voices and easing their fears. Many times they tell the quick in/quick outs things like, "Don't worry. You won't remember this when you wake up." At other times, they may accompany someone into an examination room and hold her hand during a procedure. (Sometimes this same job is done by the patient's teacher or a family member she trusts. In unusual cases, or in cases where people with a strong will or psychic sense are being worked on, an empath may be present in order to help the subject control her fear.)

One controller job that is usually done by men involves a lot of physical strength. Sometimes several men may be asked to physically grab and restrain someone so that other controllers or even empaths can work on her. Though it is common for controllers to work together, most empaths work alone except when an empath is in training and has not yet learned to master the control of wands. (For more on wands, see chapter nine.)

Controllers are called upon to lead people to certain places to keep them from wandering around a ship. More than one experiencer has told me she remembers meeting a human who was standing with little gray ETs and then walking off with him. Controllers usually lead abductees to classrooms or playrooms; when people are led by ETs, they are usually brought to examination rooms.

Empaths

One of the most important jobs done by empaths is the control of problem individuals. Sometimes a person who is not under strict control will panic, break free and run. In doing so, they can really hurt themselves and others around them. Often—especially in the case of men who tend to express their fears in a violent physical way—they try to attack the ETs, other abductees or halflings. Sometimes they run wild, looking for a way out.

When this happens on board a ship, they are in real danger. There are no locked doors, and many areas are dangerous to human life. On more than one occasion, I have seen a person being lead out of an off-limits room with awful burns. The ETs can usually heal these burns, but I have heard about people coming back from encounters with odd burns that don't heal, and I wonder if they were received in this way.

Abductees seldom get that out of hand, but when it does happen the person is restrained by controllers, or by ETs or empaths with wands (there are other ways, but these are the most common) and confined in a small, empty room until calm enough to be approached by an empath.

Sometimes, if a person is exhibiting signs of extreme anger or fear, he will be confined, even if he did not actually break away. If he were not, he would be likely to suffer many problems after his return home, and might suffer emotional damage the next time he is approached by the ETs. If a person returns home terrified, he soon perceives the ETs as life threatening. Then overwhelming anxiety sets in as his terrified subconscious waits for the next encounter.

Everyone experiences "pickup anxiety" sometimes. But these overly-stressed individuals could take it to a self-destructive extreme.

Although it would be very easy to control these people by mechanical means, doing so would not alleviate their stress. This is why working empaths are needed.

The working empath enters the room where the person is confined, and draws the dark feelings of fear and pain out of him, often replacing them with warm safe feelings. This is usually done in the following way: The empath enters the small room, usually about four feet by five feet. She approaches the subject and talks to him about what's happening and about what the ETs want from him. (See Figure 3.) Often the frightened person will see the empath as an ET. Sometimes this makes matters easier; sometimes it makes it worse. A more experienced empath will calm the subject not only with words, but also by projecting a calming, soothing color of aura at him. Less experienced workers often have a hard time radiating this calm, since they themselves are nervous.

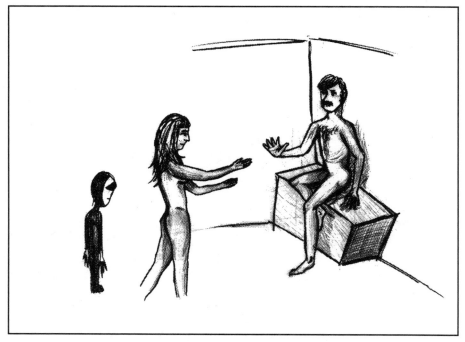

Figure 3. An empath approaching a frightened abductee.

When the empaths get close to the person, they touch him, usually on the side of the neck. If they can't get close enough, they may use a wand with a ball on it to stun him temporarily. Then, through the powers of their souls, they draw out the dark emotions from the subject.

The actual act of drawing out emotions is very hard to explain, and, in fact, is taught through symbols. The color, which is actually seen by the empath, is only a representation for the emotion behind it. The ETs teach Gemini experiencers to recognize emotions by the color (or sometimes sound) they give off to the mind's eye. For example, warm orange/pink (or harmonic tone) is comfort and peacefulness. Dark black (or discord) is deep depression or evil.

Once the empath recognizes emotions by color, she is taught to project these colors by visualizing them in her mind's eye until they can be felt.

Even the act of absorbing the colors is taught with symbolism. The act of drawing away these feelings from another is taught through the idea of eating the color and digesting it. Again, this is just symbolic. The colors are not really there, and they can't really be eaten.

After the subject's negative emotions have been drawn out, he is calm and receptive. He no longer struggles and will allow the ETs to take him home. The empath is then led away to rest. Later she is given a reward for a job well done.

The controlled subject is almost always returned home after such an event. The only exception I can remember was an unusual event I experienced some years ago.

Hetar had asked me to work with a man who had broken their control and was now in the small room. Hetar said I should be very cautious around this man because he was very strong-willed. He was a trained military man and had given the ETs quite a chase.

When I entered the room, the man jumped to his feet and started yelling obscenities at me. He even managed to pace back and forth in that small space. I let him yell and rave for a few moments. I wasn't afraid; I knew the room was being watched and the greys wouldn't allow him to harm me. Besides, if he came close enough to hit me, I would be close enough to touch him. Then I would be in control, not he. Still, I knew he was very upset and it didn't hurt either one of us to let him blow off some steam. After a short while, he must have realized how foolish he was acting, and he calmed down. (See Figure 4.)

Once he was calm, I talked to him about what was happening to him. With each few words, I came in closer until I was able to touch him. The fear in this man's soul was incredible. It was obvious to me that he was unaccustomed to the idea of not being in complete control of everything. Even so, after a while, I drew out the darkness and convinced him that the ETs only wanted to let him go home. I explained that once the door was opened, he would be taken to the gray spot on the floor across the room. Then he would awaken in his own home. And, of course, I told him "Don't worry. You won't even remember this when you wake up."

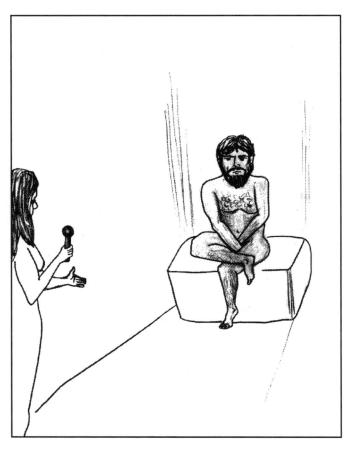

Figure 4. Michelle confronts a hostile abductee.

A common reaction of a subject after he has been worked on by an empath is to trust what the empath says without question. So he trusted me. He let the two small greys that were waiting outside the door lead him away. I was really concerned about this man and decided to watch him go home. After all, I did promise.

He really must have been a dangerous subject, because it was obvious that the greys still saw him as a threat. When he walked out of the room, they stunned him immediately. Somehow he managed to fight the effects and remained conscious enough to struggle. This must have piqued the ETs' curiosity. Instead of taking him to the gray spot, they started to drag him into an examination room. He managed to look back at me long enough to scream an obscenity at me and threaten to kill me on sight before they stunned him again. This time he stiffened and fell, limp, on the floor.

As I walked away with Hetar, I felt bad that I told the man they would be taking him right home. But how could I have known?

About two years after this event, the company I worked for hired a temporary person to work in my department. It was the man from the previous event (though, at the time, I didn't know it yet). The man and I had quite an unusual relationship. For reasons neither of us could explain, he hated me on first sight, and I was terrified that he would hurt me. Despite all that, somehow we became good friends. It seemed that we knew each other like old friends, once we got over our initial reaction. We often joked that we must have known each other in a past life. We really were not far from the truth. We didn't know it then, but we were both part of the same Secret Community.

Empaths do other types of jobs. More skilled empaths work with groups, identifying and drawing out negative emotions. Often they work with groups of other empaths who have been drawing out the darkness in panicked people.

It's not uncommon for empaths to be overcome by the dark feelings of fear given off by their subjects. Many times this darkness lingers in the empaths' own soul colors. When that happens, more experienced workers help them draw these colors out and make them inert, so that they will not suffer from their work session.

Higher levels of empaths have other uses, too. Most involve contacting the spiritual side of the experience and preparing for the future.

Full timers

The most intense level of the abduction experience is that of the full-time experiencer. This is a person of Earth origin (or at least of human form) that is, for one reason or another, a permanent resident of the ETs' world. Many of these people may be missing twins.

The missing twin syndrome [which is described in medical textbooks—Ed.] is not an uncommon occurrence for abductees. When my second child was born, she weighed just over six pounds, but the placenta was nine pounds. It was divided, as if it had developed for twins. It even had two umbilical cords. But where was the other baby? Many abductees' mothers tell stories about how the doctor insisted the abductee was going to be twins, but when the time came, the doctor was wrong.

Like everyone else in the Gemini community, full-time experiencers have jobs and relationships with the people they interact with.

The Astral Abductee

One type of abduction experience can be hard even for other experiencers to understand. This is the "alpha" or "astral" abduction. These types of abductions usually happen to people who are heavily involved in work situations with ETs and who tend to spend many nights in the company of the ETs.

The astral Gemini's soul leaves (or is taken out of) her body and transported to a host body of a person already on a ship (or in a base). Sometimes this confuses the Gemini when she's remembering in the conscious state, because the body she is put in is often that of an ET. Once she's in a host body, she does her work and then goes home to her own body.

If you are an astral experiencer, then you are probably also an empath. Though not all empaths are astral abductees, almost all astral abductees are empaths.

I should also point out that an astral abductee is likely to be a physical abductee as well. In my experiences, I have found that people who thought they were only astral abductees turn out to also be physical abductees who chose to remember only the least threatening form of the experience.

There is some controversy about this level of abduction. Some people—even some experiencers—say it's impossible. They feel that the astral abductee is only trying to hide from the fear of being physically abducted. If that is your opinion, I can only say, "You have come so far with an open mind—why slam it shut now?" Others have tried to explain astral abduction as a mind game or trick. But to experience it makes you doubt that.

Depending on your placement in the Gemini community order, this type of abduction may never happen to you—so don't worry about it.

If you don't see yourself in any of these levels of experience, don't be alarmed. I only described some of the most prevalent types of experiences that I have encountered—and, even if you are in one of these categories, the way you perceive your personal events may differ from what I have described. Besides, you may not have grown enough, or you just may not be ready to know. Still, keep trying; you'll find your place.

This is just a brief overview that could never encompass everything involved in each level of abduction. So take heart. As you move forward, you will learn more.

Hetar's words come back to me as I write this. He once said, "With knowledge comes responsibility. You must be ready to make that choice."

Sometimes, we are just not ready to make that choice. Not remembering doesn't mean we have nothing worth remembering. Sometimes it means we just are not ready to remember yet.

chapter three

Cycles of Emotion

Now that you know a little about the different levels of abduction and where you may fit into them, and now that you know that you want to take control of your experiences, what do you do? When I look back at all I had to go through to find someone who could help me, I cringe. And every time I'm contacted by someone just starting her search for personal truth, I find myself seeing the same struggle in her. Unfortunately, hardly anyone is really talking about what abductees need to know. One fellow was recently telling me that he has read more than 20 books on the subject of UFOs and not one of them had really answered his questions. Fortunately, he's involved in a decent, nurturing, supportive environment. He has other experiencers to talk to about his questions. But if there are truly as many abductees out there as I believe there are, many of you have no place to go and no one to answer your questions.

What drives you to question is what drives me to write this book and take the risk of being cast out by my family and called a "loony" by my friends. (Most of my friends know there's something different about me, but very few know what it actually is.) Something inside us compels us to do what we are doing. We feel a burning need to know what's happening—and sometimes to tell about what we know. We switch from feeling obsessed by the little internal voice that pushes us forward, to being totally convinced that we don't need to know anything. This is one of the cycles we abduction experiencers endure.

You have probably already recognized what I mean by cycles. There's a very definite pattern to the way abductees are "allowed" to do things, particularly when it comes to discovering who we are. These patterns can also be described as a series of cycles. Just about every experiencer I have spoken with experiences these cycles in one form or another.

Sometimes an abductee's cycles are so dramatic that they stretch across extremes. An example is the person who is picked up and worked on without his conscious memory. This starts a cycle of dreams and night terrors. As his subconscious mind tries to explain the event to its conscious counterpart, the cycle grows, and he may become afraid of the dark or of being alone. Even if he does not believe in "UFOs" or "aliens," he may start believing something is happening to him. If he discusses his feelings with a friend (or spouse), the friend probably will tell him that he is only dreaming or imagining it, and the cycle will begin to wane. Without further stimulus, he will begin to believe it was just a dream. The fear will subside little by little, until it fades from memory and finally goes away. The experiencer's life seems back to normal—but only until the next time he or she is abducted and the cycle starts again.

If you regularly find yourself trying to rationalize strange, very real dreams that you feel are somehow more than just dreams, and you say things like "I have to stop watching so much TV" or "No more pizza before bedtime," there's a good chance you are experiencing this cycle.

Sometimes, the person experiencing this cycle finds that the memories seem more vivid and fade more slowly with each repeat cycle, until the memories are no longer fading, and he is compelled to get help. Then he may fall into a new cycle that I call "the need-to-know cycle."

People experiencing the need-to-know cycle often feel burning compulsions to know everything and anything about their experiences. They read, they go to lectures, they do just about anything that they feel will bring them closer to understanding what's happening to them. The real cycling starts when they become overwhelmed by something they read or see and withdraw from everything connected with the abduction experience. They may even throw away their books and swear never to think about the subject again. Sooner or later they calm down and can face the subject again. That's when the obsession kicks in again and the passion to know takes over their lives. So the cycle turns around—and, before they know it, they are in the thick of things again.

Of course, not everyone experiences cycles of the same intensity, and not everyone experiences every cycle.

Another common cycle deals with the inability to understand the information given by ETs. People stuck in this cycle alternate between feeling scared and unsure about what they discover is happening to them, and feeling privileged and important. Many go from feeling like lab animals used in some horrible experiment to feeling like much loved pets or cherished children, then back to feeling like lab rats again. These cycles are confusing—not only to the abductees, but also to their support people. This is especially true if the support people are not experiencers.

Abductees living through these cycles can be very involved in their own worlds, and may not even see the pattern of their cycles. We can truly believe that the part of the cycle we are living through is real, and has never happened to us before. But the people around us see it differently.

A woman I know is experiencing the cycle described above. One week she talks about ETs as if they are hideously mad scientists. The next week, she relates a wonderful time she remembers with them. Depending on when I talk to her, she's either a victim, a volunteer or everything in between. But there's nothing wrong with her. She is just fighting to make sense of an incredibly complex series of events that she has only partial memory of. In one part of her mind, it all makes sense, and she's content; in the other, it's all terrible and beyond reason.

Cycles are caused by many different factors. Some of the factors that make us cycle are:

1. The elapsed time between abduction events and when we remember them.

It's not uncommon for a person to have something happen that triggers a memory that's years old. For example, I was sitting here writing this book when my daughter came up behind me and lightly pulled my hair. For that split second I was not in my chair anymore. I was in bed, and an ET was tugging at my hair to wake me. The actual event happened some time ago, but it felt like it just happened at that moment.

2. The attitude of others around us.

If the people in your life are very negative about what you are experiencing and give you a hard time—or if you happen to be living in an area of the country that's being bombarded with the "UFO media blitz," you will have a much harder time discovering what you truly feel.

3. Many of us have a sense of when our next visit will happen.[1]

You may have had at least the passing feeling that you will be "working" tonight (as I like to put it), or that the ETs are around somewhere nearby, just waiting to come get you. Maybe you have decided to stay home instead of driving alone one night, or found an excuse to have someone else stay with you so you wouldn't have to be alone for just that reason. Don't be embarrassed by it. I think we have all done it at one time or another.

As that time draws near, pickup anxiety sets in, and we once again find ourselves wide awake in the wee hours, jumping at every sound, our heads swimming in fear, our hearts pounding so hard it hurts. Fear can cause all kinds of responses, most of which are not very good for you in the long run, so it's important to break the cycles that cause you to fear.

Besides being very damaging to you, these cycles can drive the people around you crazy. Your friends or spouse will probably see these cycles before you do. You should talk to them about it and try to realize that going in cycles is neither a productive direction nor, necessarily, your fault. You didn't choose to have these emotional cycles, but you are the one who must deal with them. It's going to be hard. Most of the people I know who are caught in cycles cannot even see them until they actually break them.

I was the same way (and to some point, I still am). I just didn't believe I was caught in a cycle, no matter what my husband or best friend said. Even when a professional UFO researcher pointed out my cycles, I couldn't see them. I would say, "I know it sounds the same, but this time it's totally different." My husband would throw his hands up in the air and say he was giving up. (I'm glad he never really meant it.)

After a few cycles, I decided to start writing down everything I was feeling in a journal of emotions. Then when my husband or friends pointed out I was cycling again, I went back to my book. Sure enough, they were right. I had come full circle. I was using different words, but saying the same thing.

---

1. I have found this to be the most prominent factor.—ML

With that new knowledge, I was able to confront my cycles and for the most part, break them. After they were broken, I could move forward again, back on my road to discovery. You can do so, too.

If you or those around you think you are caught in a cycle, you should first try to recognize what is causing you to cycle and take steps to overcome any unproductive cycles before they become hard habits to break. This can be done by following a few simple steps:

1. Keep a log or journal of all your feelings.
Write, draw or even scribble down all your memories and feelings about your experiences in a journal and keep it in a safe place. If you feel odd writing about things like ETs or UFOs, make up a simple code for these things. You may want to call the ETs something like "the Smiths," and you can write to yourself about your visit with the Smiths. If anyone finds the book, she will never know the Smiths aren't human unless you tell her.

2. Listen to yourself talk.
When you talk to others about your experiences, take the time to listen to what you say. I know this sounds strange, but the fact is, most people seldom listen to what they themselves say and how they say it. After a while, you'll find that you often answer your questions as you ask them.

Other things that will help you break out of cycles are a little more involved. You have to look at—and deal with—what you are afraid of. You have to learn about your personal experiences, and you have to develop a sense of self-worth that you may be lacking if you have been living the life of the victim.

Don't be afraid of finding out your life is running in cycles. It doesn't mean there is anything wrong with you. Actually, it means you are a strong person—strong because you can live with something others couldn't even imagine, and even when it overwhelms you and you have to turn your back on it, you come back and face it again. You are strong because you are making the effort to focus your life and discover what's really going on around you, and because you will come out of this with a whole understanding of the universe in terms many people could not even dream of.

chapter four

Getting Help

OK, so you are hard at work, trying to break the unproductive cycles, and you are starting to feel a little stronger. Now you feel it's time to get "outside" help.

I have heard it said, and I'm sure you have too, that once a person realizes she has a problem, the hardest part of the battle is over. But if you have run up against the wall of confusion and bad help out there, you know that is not entirely true when it comes to the abduction experience.

I experienced great difficulty when I started looking for help for myself. If you have already started looking for help from others, you know what I mean. It can prove to be the most emotionally upsetting event of your life. For some, it turns out to be much more damaging to their sense of self than any encounter with ETs ever was.

Sometimes you may feel like there's no right thing to do. Sometimes you may feel as if the only way to go is down. Often you may feel alone. That's why you need someone to help you along the way, if only for an occasional "reality" check, to let you know you are not insane.

It is beyond the imagination of the average Joe Public to understand the complex problems and dynamics of what people involved with these "travelers" experience when they are alone and unsupported. But even worse than having no help is seeking help, trusting those you find, and being hurt by them.

This happens more often than most people running support groups would like to admit, but it has to be said. You have to be provided with information so you may learn from the mistakes of those who have gone before you.

But paramount to all is what Hetar told me about a need that has to be filled. There are people like me and you who are hungry for this knowledge and ready to be fed. There are people out there who need to know, but have no one to question. And there are people out there who will tell you that they know all the answers—but they don't.

Not all help is good help. As a matter of fact, sometimes what seems like good help can, in fact, be very unproductive. There are other things that can be helpful for a while, but when their usefulness comes to an end, you have to move on or they can be quite hurtful.

Now that you have decided that you need to seek help (I assume you already have if you are reading this), I feel for you. What you have in the window ahead of you is the hardest view you'll ever look at. It's a picture that will shake up your world. But you must remember, it is not a view you have never seen before. As a matter of fact, this view is something you are very familiar with. In this reality, however, you choose, for many reasons, to keep the window shade drawn and closed tight. But if you are curious enough and have enough strength and determination to pull the shade aside, you will be on your way through that window to the new horizon beyond it.

I must warn you, however: Think good and hard before you attempt to move that shade because it will change your life forever. Not a little change. A big one. A very big one.

You are going to grow beyond belief. Sometimes people grow so much that they lose touch with their former lives. Some people experience such events in their lives that they feel as if their whole world has been destroyed—only to be rebuilt in a different way. Some outgrow relationships with family and spouses (especially if the relationships were weak and shaky to begin with). Many even lose faith in their religions.

On the other hand, a lot of experiencers have found that the events of their life have strengthened their bonds with loved ones and solidified their faith. Many have found explanations for long misunderstood problems and were able to resolve them.

So you must ask yourself: Are you ready for those types of changes? Are you ready for the strain? Don't kid yourself—it is an extreme strain.

If you easily answered "yes" to both questions, then take more time to contemplate what they mean and what possible changes could happen in your life. When you are not sure if you are ready, but your heart is burning for knowledge so badly you can taste it, then it is probably a good time to begin your discovery.

If you ignore the burning hunger, you will starve, and your life will be nothing but hollow. An experiencer I know said, "If you don't keep trying, you are giving up a career as a movie star to work in a shoe store." Her words were figurative, but oh, so true.

You see, if you are hungry for knowledge—if the passion to discover who you are is in you—you must be fed. But you must be very careful where you go to be fed.

Here are a few things to keep in mind:

1. No matter how faithful you are to your religion, do not bring your concerns to the clergy.

Too many times, the close-minded views that the clergy of most major religions hold about humans and the universe cause them to doubt what you tell them. No matter how much they want to believe you, they have to base their decisions on the doctrines of their religion.

Based on the experiences of many I have spoken to who have taken this route, the clergy can only come as far as believing you believe what you say, but you are obviously mentally ill. This is because the doctrines of their church say the types of things abductees experience don't happen.

One woman I know made the mistake of telling her fundamentalist Baptist minister about her suspicions of alien abduction, hoping he could give her some support and sympathy. However, he couldn't, because in his belief system, extraterrestrials simply don't exist, and her experiences could only be explained one way. He believed the ETs the woman saw where demons. So instead of getting support, the woman was declared "demon possessed" and the minister performed a public exorcism. Later, when she told him the alien encounters were still happening despite the exorcism, he said that she was obviously evil and told her to leave the church's flock and never come back. Not only was the poor woman still having problems with the ETs she couldn't understand, but now her faith in her church was destroyed

What happened to this experiencer was an extreme, but it's not unique. Many experiencers are forced to live under inappropriate labels given to them by others.

Even if you don't believe your own pastor, priest, or rabbi would react so heartlessly, you must understand that they are keepers of their particular written faiths, and what you have to tell them could be seen as a threat to those faiths.

2. Not all counselors, psychologists and psychiatrists are open to this phenomenon.

Even though the general public may seem open to the experience, it is still not readily accepted as a valid experience by many people in the psychiatric profession. Some psychiatrists, psychologists and counselors believe the abduction experience is just the mind's way of covering childhood sexual abuse. (I have talked to several professionals on this subject, and not one has seen an abductee that is using ETs to screen sexual abuse.)

Some doctors believe the abduction experience is a psychosis in itself. They feel that the same type of sickness that makes a person believe he is Napoleon or Julius Caesar can make someone believe he is an alien abductee.

I don't need to prove to you that abduction is real. I just need to warn you about people who may never believe you, and who may try to force you into the mold of mental sickness. If it were to happen to you, you would not be the first person to go through years of therapy for something like sexual abuse without results. Sometimes this type of therapy has even made some people feel worse.

If you do decide to contact a therapist, be careful. Not all doctors or therapists who are open to abduction phenomena are in the therapy business to help you. Some are in it for their own gain and don't care about the abductees.

Here are a few good rules to follow when choosing a therapist or doctor, particularly if you plan to undergo hypnosis to remember your experiences.

1. Don't be afraid to ask questions.

As abductees living in a world of skeptics, we are accustomed to having to make people believe us. Sometimes we want someone to believe us so badly that we jump into things with our eyes closed.

Ask about training, references, charges (some therapists charge; some do not). Ask if the charges are billed to your health insurance under another diagnosis (and what that diagnosis will be). Depending on what type of job you have, a doctor's diagnosis could have an effect on your career. But most of all, ask about follow-up support. Does the doctor run a support group? Is there a fee for the group? Is there a person available between group meetings to talk to if you feel the need? (Even at 3:00 in the morning, when you really need to talk to someone?)

If you don't like the answers you get, check out another doctor. Don't rush into something you feel dissatisfied with just because you are hungry for answers.

2. If you undergo hypnosis, make sure you get transcripts of the session.

Transcripts are very helpful when you are trying to sort out what you experienced, compared to what you actually said to the doctor. Many abductees—myself included—have been surprised by what we chose to verbally express during our hypnosis sessions compared to what we remember experiencing. Also, transcripts can help you understand what others saw happening during a regression, not just what you saw from your inside view. This can make for a much more complete picture.

Some doctors and therapists may ask you to pay a small fee for the photocopying or tapes, but they shouldn't refuse you access to your records. They are your medical records, and you have a right to them. You may even suggest bringing your own tape recorder to a session.

Never sign a release for the doctor to have exclusive rights to use your experiences for his upcoming TV special or book unless you have it checked over by someone who knows what you are signing. This will prevent you from accidentally signing away your own rights to talk about your experiences.

3. Ask questions about any support group before you go.

Before you enter those doors, make sure you know whether it is truly a support group you are entering, or a doctor's study group. The difference is clear when you look at the purpose of both groups. A support group's primary goal is to provide a supportive environment where experiencers can gather to explore and share their experiences. A study group's primary goal is to provide an interactive situation a researcher can observe and study.

This might not seem like a big difference, but it really is. I once attended a study group in the hope of talking to other abductees about things that were troubling me, and I was simply overwhelmed by the meeting. The therapist in charge was in a position of studying the people and didn't want to interfere with the topic of discussion. Twenty or so people were in the room. Someone started talking about the messages of Mary and how they related to the messages she received from the ETs. Another experiencer disagreed, and said the messages of the Hindu texts were more accurate. The two of them began an argument. After more than 40 minutes of their arguing, I got up and left, feeling very empty.

In a true support environment, the arguing would have been controlled, and the meeting would have been more productive for everyone there who wanted to talk, but never got the chance.

The first few times you walk into any group, you are likely to be nervous. That is only natural. Remember that the other people around you are nervous, too. We experiencers are all linked together, so you are likely to feel different in a room full of experiencers than you have felt anywhere else in your life. But that does not mean you will feel at home right away.

After your nerves settle, you should feel a sense of community. If you don't, then think about the group and your part in it. If you find that you return home from group meetings with a heavy, sick feeling in your heart or feeling like it just wasn't the place for you, then the place isn't for you.

Hetar was right when he told me, "When you are home, you'll know it. No one will have to tell you." It's true. Trust your heart and not your head in matters of this nature. We were all given a sixth sense to protect us from harm. You have this in you, and you should learn to trust it so you will know good help from bad.

You have to find people who will nurture you, not people who only want to sap you dry. And be cautious of those who only want to know your experiences for their own benefit—not just doctors doing research, but also friends who may think what you have to tell them is more exciting than ghost stories around a campfire. Remember, when you are sitting up at 2:30 in the morning, shaking in fear as you remember and relive what you told them about earlier that day, they will be home in their nice, safe beds, sound asleep, thinking, "Better her than me."

4. Don't let everything around you get too heavy.

I am reminded of something time and time again: the importance of play. We have to remember to relax and play. We work all day and most nights, sometimes cramming a week or more of time into one night. We are learning about and coping with things that are very confusing and stressful, so we have to unwind. Maybe you don't remember all the things you are doing with the ETs, but your subconscious does—and so does your body. The tension of your work has to be released through play. Play is also the best way we have to explore ourselves and the people around us. So keep playing, and be healthy.

Figure 5. Experiencers dancing behind an ET.

chapter five

Childhood Experiences

The idea of play brings me to a related topic—that is children. After all, children play. They are not afraid of playing, and they are never embarrassed by it.

Experiencers don't have to be reminded that the whole abduction experience seems to revolve around children in many different ways. We have all seen and interacted with infants and children, and many people remember being treated and talked to like a child by the ETs, no matter how old they are.

This is probably because most of us started with the ETs on or even before our births. You may recall seeing ETs as a small child and being unafraid. Most people do not develop fear until they are taught Earth reasoning. It is only when we are told (perhaps indirectly) that these things do not happen or are wrong that we begin to fear.

The way you react to the experiences you had as a child has a lot to do with your current perception of events. Let's talk about some of the experiences from my past and the past of some of the people I work with. Whether or not these things have happened to you, these examples should give you an idea of what I mean by reactions back then relating to your perceptions now.

An experiencer friend and I were talking about our childhoods. She mentioned the first time she remembers seeing a halfling as a child. She was in a playroom all alone. A tall gray being led a halfling boy about her same age into the room. The grey told her the halfling was her brother and she should play with him for a while. She panicked. She was afraid of the little boy. She actually believed he was her real, earthbound brother, and that the ETs had done something awful to deform him.

To this day, some of her most difficult memories to face are those dealing with halflings. The fears formed early in our lives are often the hardest to manage.

I experienced an almost identical event. When the little halfling boy was led to me, however, I knew the grey did not mean he was my brother from back on my Earth home. (He may, indeed, have come from part of my family's genetic base, though.) My reaction to him was quite different from the reaction my friend had. I thought he looked very thin and sick, with only scant hair and a pale, hollow face. I took pity on him and gave him a lot of attention. I remember that we played for a long time. And, although he did not really seem to understand what I was trying to do at times, we had fun.

As a result of this positive experience as a child, I have no problems working with halflings. I seem to work with halflings quite often.

Another example of perception can be found in a little girl and boy I know who are both abductees themselves. The little girl talks about taking rides in the sky with "father." She is not afraid, and even talks openly about the medical examinations. On the other hand, the little boy (who is about the same age) is so upset by the experience that he doesn't even like to see people wearing dark sunglasses. When you ask him why, he says he doesn't know.

Many abductees have recalled experiencing the following as children: The child experiencer is led to a playground and is allowed to play with the equipment (slides, swings, the usual playground things). After a little while, the ETs return with some halfling children. The abductee is instructed to teach them how to work the equipment. Sometimes the child is told to teach the little hybrid children how to "have fun" or "to play." In my case, the instruction was to teach them how to have "happy play." These simple types of tasks are often requested of child experiencers.

Many times children remember holding hands in a circle and levitating around the room. Sometimes they sing with the greys or are asked to come and dance with the grey in the center of the room. (See Figure 6.) These actions are reinforced with words of praise and love. Children are encouraged to feel that they belong in a family with the aliens. They are also told repeatedly that they are, in fact, aliens in human form. This last statement probably does not surprise you.

When I questioned a group of about 40 lifelong abductees who were experiencing different levels of remembrance and fear, all except one admitted believing that somehow they were aliens in human form.

Figure 6. "Come dance with me."

This brings me to another point of interest. Many people involved in encounters—particularly those in the upper levels of experiences—believe that they contracted to do this work with the ETs when they were very young. Some even believe this took place before they were born. Many people researching this experience see themselves in a pre-human situation.

My discovery of this came during my hypnotic regression. While under hypnosis, I told the doctor that this (what I do for them) is my job. It was what I always promised to do. He asked me how long ago I made this promise. I said a long, long time ago. He asked if it was when I was a baby, and I answered that it was before that. When I awoke, I was very aware of a long-time, pre-birth commitment to this effort.

If you don't feel this commitment, don't be surprised. It's one of those things that only seems to come after the fear is under control. Some people, especially quick in/quick outs, never discover it.

All in all, your childhood abduction experiences were probably less traumatic than your adult experiences, if only because as a child you did not know how different you were from the others around you. But then again, as children, we are all the same. And, in the scheme of the universe, we are all just children. Our world is merely a universal nursery school, and we, the people of Earth, are the little children. We are given only one lesson to learn in this school—a very simple lesson, in theory. We must learn to love, unconditionally, without limitation and without question. We must learn to love not just people, but all things. After all, all things are part of the same eternity. And though it seems like a big order to take, it is a must. But I don't have to tell you that; they already did.

chapter six

Living in Fear

I know that everything I have said so far is very difficult to take to heart if you are living in the stages of fear. Fear is a very hurtful thing, and of all the things that can happen to you in your human existence, half memories of alien encounters can be the most terrifying. Nothing I can think of that can happen to the average Joe Public can compare to what is happening to you now, especially if you are only remembering bits and pieces. And you probably know by now that there is no way you can stop this from happening to you.

When the fear is at its worst, you may find yourself not sleeping much. When you do try, you might even want to sleep with the lights on or a gun under your pillow. You may be terrified of being alone or of taking drives around any area not busy with people. Nightmares and anxiety may follow you, particularly when you are alone.

These are all very normal reactions, and they pass slowly as you explore your experiences. When you are living through the fear, however, no words on paper can ease you. It has to come from inside of you.

Most of your greatest fears come from your not knowing the whats, whens and whys. As you answer these questions, you will become less and less afraid.

I wish I could tell you that the fear will go away quickly, but it is a long process. It can creep up on you every now and then, no matter how much you understand. (Unfortunately, none of us will ever know everything.) These episodes of fear are usually triggered by something. If you can find out what your triggers are, you can either control them or avoid them.

If you sit anxiously, waiting to be scared, you are only hurting the quality of your life. I have to tell you, "Don't be afraid of the fear." Those are Hetar's words again—and they are very true.

His words were prompted by an event that occurred in the spring of 1991. I was sitting up at night, after my husband and children were asleep in bed. One of my favorite times of the week is my Saturday night. Usually, sometime after midnight, when the house is dark and quiet, I come downstairs wrapped in a blanket, plug in my headphones and put on my favorite music. Then I sit back in my rocking chair and relax. Sometimes I just sit and listen, but once in a while I get involved in the music and mouth the words as if I were singing along.

On that night, I was sitting in my chair with my headphones on and my eyes closed, hamming it up, when someone softly but firmly touched my arm. I was startled, expecting to see my husband standing there laughing at me. Instead, my eyes made contact with two deep, dark, lens-covered eyes and the face of a small gray ET. I was washed with shock, then resignation. I got up, quietly took his hand, and walked over with him out of the living room, into the kitchen, through the kitchen table (yes, I said *through*) and out of the closed window toward the source of the blue light.

For a long time after that night, my shock and surprise stayed with me. I became very nervous and was terrified to listen to my music at night. (Doing so had been one of my greatest ways to relax after a hard week with work and the kids, and I was truly suffering from its absence.) But no matter how hard I tried, I just could no longer bring myself to relax with music. When I tried, I would sit there with the room lights on. I could not even close my eyes. I would stare at the windows in the kitchen, unable to pull my eyes away. My tension grew. I did not want to be startled again. If they were coming, I was going to *see* them coming. One time, I even called my husband to come downstairs and get me because I was too afraid to go upstairs alone, just in case they were up there waiting for me. I grew afraid to do anything because I was afraid I would become scared. I was even reluctant to close the bathroom door at night. I feared that they might be standing there when I opened it.

It just destroyed my life, until Hetar sat down with me and told me about fear. He helped me separate my real fears from unnecessary fears. With that in mind, I was able to let go of the fear and grow.

There are certain fears you may have about the ETs that you never have to lose sleep over because they simply won't happen. They are the following:

1. "The ETs will kill me, or fail to bring me home again."

This just isn't done. You are on Earth for a reason. If they didn't bring you back to Earth, you'd never be able to fulfill that reason—and they know that.

2. "I will come back with something missing or put together wrong."

I have heard experiencers say, "Ever since they worked on my spine I have had the worse backaches," or "They did something to my ovaries, and the next week I developed a cyst." I remember thinking that my asthma worsened after they removed my lungs. This is only a matter of perception.

Many people I know would prefer to blame every problem in their life on the ETs. But the truth is that the procedures they do seldom, if ever, leave anything more than a white scar or some light bleeding. Many times it is our perceptions that cause us to connect our problems with ET interaction.

For example, my asthma had worsened dramatically in the past 24 months, and I did remember the "lung" event about two years ago. But when I investigated further, I found that the incident had actually occurred more than seven years ago. Somehow, I connected the worsening of my asthma to the more traumatic event, rather than to the fact that the pollen count in New England had been unusually high during the past two summers and my asthma is allergy-induced.

The woman with the cyst had drawn a similar conclusion. The procedure that she had recently remembered happened much more than a year before the cyst showed up. She never took into consideration that the women in her family have a history of ovarian cysts and that not everyone in her family is an abductee.

When you are afraid, it is easy to blame things on what you fear.

Once in a great while, someone does have a very bad, long-term side effect. Many experiencers' sinus passages are scarred from repeatedly undergoing implant procedures. Also, remember what can happen to people who panic and run to areas where they are exposed to danger. I was told that one of the burns these people suffer is very difficult to repair. And another Gemini assures me that staring at a particular light in a dangerous room will cause blindness that the greys cannot repair.

If you feel that the ETs have damaged you in any way, you should tell them so. They'll try to fix it, provided it really is their mistake. Please understand, I am not advocating calling ETs instead of your earth doctor. Always get help from your earth doctor first, but it doesn't hurt to tell ETs as well.

Sometimes pregnant women fear that the ETs will take their babies away. I was very concerned about this. I questioned Hetar about it. He told me that they never take what they have not put there. He would go no further. After the unusual birth of my daughter, I questioned Hetar about missing twins. (See Chapter 2.) He repeated that they don't take away anything they didn't put there. Then he mysteriously said, "May your child be as happy as mine."

3. "The ETs will hurt the people I love to control my actions."

ETs do not need to hold your family members hostage in order to make you behave or perform. They can make you behave by many other ways. This fear comes from the misunderstanding on the part of the experiencer with partial memories.

Since the abduction phenomenon usually runs in families, your family members will often be present when you are there. Sometimes, out of fear, you misinterpret your memories and feel as if they are being used against you. Another personal example explains what I mean.

I have memories of working with a large, console-like machine that streams an electric-type current through me, causing numbness in one half of my body. As the intensity grows, I become very uncomfortable. Hetar is always there at these times. He tells me to hold on and wait. Finally, when the sensation is such that I think it's going to kill me, he tells me, "Push back." I do push back, and force all the energy back into the machine, where I presume it's measured.

Every few times I work with this machine, the intensity is raised in order to build up my strength, in much the same way that a body builder increases the amount of weights he lifts each time. When the effort gets too difficult and I'm obviously having a hard time, he leads one of my children into the room and tells me to concentrate on her so I can maintain my control.

Before I was fully aware of these memories, I was sure that they were bringing my child in as a threat. ("Do what I want, or I'll hurt your child.") Now I know that was not the case. As that memory filled in, I remembered that Hetar would bring my child in and tell me to concentrate on the child so I could maintain my control. He was not threatening me; he was giving me a focal point.

4. "The ETs will abduct everyone who spends time with me."

What will happen to a friend or spouse who happens to be with you when ETs pick you up? Worrying about this is pointless. If that friend or spouse is a significant, well-woven part of your life, chances are good that this has already happened to him—and he's just fine, isn't he? You cannot stop making friends and loving people to protect them from the ETs. If you do, you are going to be unhappy all your life.

On many occasions, friends and spouses are simply "turned off" when the greys come for you. They are simply made to fall very quickly into a deep sleep. It's like being unconscious (with no ill effects that I'm aware of). When you return, your friends are allowed to wake up and are totally unaware that anything has happened at all.

A few nights ago, I was in bed talking to my husband. It was very late at night. After a few minutes, there was a lull in the conversation. When I spoke again, my husband did not respond. He was completely unconscious. At that moment, I realized that the room was filling with blue light. A small grey walked through my closed bedroom door. (Now that's an annoying habit! I may never get used to seeing them walk through closed doors. It seems they have a flair for the theatrical, because if the door is open, they'll walk through the wall next to it.) In the morning, my husband had absolutely no idea that anything had happened.

Also, you should not fear that the ETs will turn someone off while he is driving, thus causing the car to wreck. That doesn't happen either. If they are coming to get someone while he is in a car, the driver may have an uncontrollable urge to pull over and stop the car, or the car will be stopped by a light beam from the ship. The car will be returned to the road later.

They usually put subjects back on the road right where they got them. Sometimes they put them back on the road farther along where they would have been had they not stopped (provided they can do that without too much trouble). Once in a while, they may put them down somewhere totally different.

I was in a car with two friends, heading west on the Massachusetts Turnpike. A few minutes later (or so it seemed) we saw toll booths in front of us. This did not seem too odd, since the road we were on had toll booths on each exit. We assumed that somehow we took a wrong turn and were leaving the highway by mistake. Then we realized that the toll booths we were approaching were halfway to the White Mountains in New Hampshire, more than fifty miles away! There was no way we could have gone that far into New Hampshire without knowing it. For that matter, there was no way we could have gotten off the turnpike without passing the exit booths—unless we had taken an unexpected ride with the little gray guys.

Oddly enough, even though I knew we had missing time, I never thought anything about it and neither did my friends. (Sounds familiar? Not being concerned about missing time is one of the classic signs of the abduction experience.)

5. Pickup anxiety.

The most common fear experienced by Gemini people is what I call "pickup anxiety." I cannot begin to tell you how many experiencers have told me, "If only they would knock on the door, I'd go with them in a flash" or "If they would ask me instead of just appearing in my bedroom and grabbing me, I'd be happy to go."

The only way to overcome the fear of being picked up by surprise is to realize that you are experiencing it. Many people confuse pickup anxiety with fear of the whole event. One hint that you may be suffering from pickup anxiety is if you sleep with the light or the TV on. Another good sign is if you wake up at night and are afraid to open your eyes for fear of seeing "them" stand there.

After you become aware that you are having pickup anxiety, resolve to tell the ETs the next time they pick you up that you are scared of the stunning effect. But be prepared to commit to a non-defensive posture. Remember that when they approach a human, they have no way of telling what the person's reactions will be. You have to remember that the average human is almost twice the height and three times the weight of the average ET. Even a simple reflex (such as swinging your arms in front of your face) could cause some injury if an ET were standing too close and were taken by surprise.

Maybe you live in a busy apartment building. What if you were to scream out at the sight of the ETs and someone were to run to your aid? She would not be able to find you in the apartment, even though you had just screamed. Your spouse would have a lot of explaining to do. Or what if you were to panic and hurt yourself?

So, for many reasons, the majority of experiencers are rendered suddenly and completely immobile until the ETs are sure they won't panic. (It seems that after arriving on board the ships, the Gemini people's memories return, and they are no longer scared. But quick in/quick outs may still be quite frightened.) However, like all living things, people are unpredictable, and for a variety of reasons, anyone can panic or lose control. Remember the job of the controllers and empaths. They would not be needed if everyone who calmed down remained calm.

6. "I will come to love the ETs."

Another fear I'd like to address at this time, and it's a very important thing to talk about though you might not be ready to explore this area yet, is the fear of the love.

If as you read these next few pages and you find yourself saying "That's crap" or "I can't believe that," please skip through it to fear #8. You can always come back to it later when you are ready. I know you'll come back to it. Maybe not for a while, but you will, someday in the future. So…here it goes.

One of the hardest fears for us to face as human-raised, earth-bound individuals with jobs, families, bills and troubles comes from discovering (and most of us do) that we have an emotional relationship with these ETs. It's a scary thing to wake up one day and realize that you have incredibly deep feelings for a "creature" whom you are actively fearing (and perhaps hating) at the time. But this does happen.

It is an unmistakable, undeniable fact that we, over the course of our lives, build strong loving relationships with these odd little beings. It's also very true that many of the people I know who spoke about ETs with fear and contempt at the start of their journey now talk about them more favorably as they explore their experiences more deeply.

Hetar is more to me than a keeper or handler. He's my teacher, my brother, my lover, my friend. He and I have a relationship as deep as any other I have achieved in this life. I don't have to tell you how trying this can be for my husband.

This does not mean that I never get angry at Hetar. I do. But I could never hate him or wish him harm. He is part of me. He has been a part of me for as long as I have been who I am—just as your mentor is a part of you.

You see, my relationship with Hetar is far from unique. It is proving to be the norm with people I know. The depth of the relationship each one of us has with his or her teacher depends greatly on the depth of his or her total experience. One could not expect a one-time abductee to have any relationship with the ETs at all.

These relationships are real. I have found that many times the greatest fear stopping a person from growing is that of admitting, even to herself, that she can have such feeling for a being that her conscious intellect (and the media around her) tells her is so different, so alien. After all, we live in a world where we find it hard to tolerate those who are only slightly different from ourselves.

This fear can be so overpowering that it stops one's growth dead in its tracks. One person in my company of experiencer friends told me, "I'd rather be dead than to be their friends." She cannot understand my positive attitude—but that's fine. I can understand what she is going through. I felt much the same way once. My feelings were not so extreme, however—perhaps because I have always had more active conscious memories, so this whole thing wasn't a shock to me. Still, negative emotions pass as one digs deeper into her experiences and learns how comfortable she truly is in the company of the ETs.

One time I was working with a young boy. I was showing him the pictures of the other place (a world that we Geminis are often told stories about and frequently explore with the help of a series of small memory spheres). Hetar came to tell me it was just about time for me to go home. I left the child with my assistant and walked away with Hetar. (This event didn't happen on the ship. We were in a stationary base, which I believe is under the desert in the Southwest.)

As we walked down the hallway, Hetar asked me how I felt. I told him I was very tired. I had been working all night, and I felt it was going to be hard for me to go home and care for my children all day without any rest. I really needed some sleep. He said it was all right. He could arrange it for me. He stopped another tall grey and spoke to him for a moment, then we walked through the halls until we came to his room. Once there, I curled up in bed with him. He put his arms around me and told me he was proud of the good job I do for him and that he loves me. I fell asleep and awoke later, well rested. (I have no idea how long I slept.) Hetar sent me back home on a small ship. As he had promised, time was bent. I got home well before sunup.

7. "I may have had sex with an ET."

Another thing that may scare you, especially if your memories are only sketchy or if you are a quick in/quick out, is that on more than one occasion our mentors are our lovers in a very real sense. Hetar and I have shared sexual pleasures several times. Each event was an act of either love or initiation (and quite different from other events, during which the sexual act is mimicked during an experiment or an act of dominance).

Many people reading this will find themselves saying "Thank God, I'm not the only one. I'm not really crazy." I have heard that reaction before. This sexual side of the experience is one of the things we usually remember, but just cannot bring ourselves to ask other people about because we fear they might consider us "perverts."

I have been told by some experiencers that the ETs do not have the proper sex organs to have intercourse with humans. Yet, I remember the experience very clearly—as do many others I know. I spoke to an ET on the subject recently. She told me that even though they lack the proper, human sex organs, they can create a very real facsimile of the sex act. I said, "Then it doesn't really happen?" She said, "That's a matter of perception. If you believe it happens, then it's reality to you, isn't it?" So did I really have sex with Hetar? It's a matter of subjective reality. In my reality I did. In his, who knows?

Once you accept that you are an experiencer, the fear of discovering that this type of thing may be happening to you *with* your consent can be the hardest thing for you to face.

Someone once proposed to me that all of the emotional attachment comes from the fear response, in much the same way an abused child tends to cling to the abusing parent. But I think that once you have explored your personal experiences, you will find that to be untrue.

Let me give you one more example to illustrate how you can be held back by the fear of discovering you have feelings for an ET. A woman in one of my groups has a position in the psychiatric field, and is well respected by her friends and colleagues. She had experienced what she felt were astral abductions for a good part of her life, but believed she had no physical contact with ETs. Throughout most of her life, she had seen the tall, blond, human-like aliens that are often seen with the greys. She has also had many events where she would see the blonds with "animals."

The animals were not really "animals." They were gray beings. The woman assumed that her mind chose to see them as animals because their actual form was so different that it would scare her.

After a lot of thought, questions and compelling dreams, she underwent hypnosis, and discovered that she had been experiencing actual physical abductions. She also discovered she had no problem seeing the gray ETs in their actual forms. Oddly enough, they didn't scare her at all. What she found most surprising was not that she was having physical abductions, but that she was experiencing deep feelings of love and companionship with a tall gray being she was interacting with. He held her and comforted her after a rather draining procedure. When she was told it was time to go, she cried. She didn't want to leave him. Her subconscious wasn't stopping her from remembering the faces of the greys in her memory to save her from fear, but to stop her from the sadness and longing to be with them. Her discovery also answered the question of why she had never really felt totally at home anywhere she had ever lived on Earth.

8. "Others around me will think that I'm crazy."

Discovering these new things about yourself doesn't mean you need to stand on the highest mountain and shout them to the world. Just be confident in the messages of your heart and be patient. Some people will always disbelieve you. After all, some people still won't believe the world is round. It is not necessary for you to convince them.

That you believe you is important; that your brother-in-law believes you is not.

If the person you love most cannot believe you, don't force him. Just let him know you feel very strongly about this and ask him not to let his skepticism prevent you from discovering what you are going through. Allow him to ask questions, no matter how stupid you might think the questions are. It's important that they get honest answers. If you don't know an answer to a question, tell them that.

Be sure to make the difference clear between things that you know happened and things that you are not yet sure of.

Try to keep in mind that, no matter how hungry you get for answers, no matter how obsessed you become with the need to know, you still have loved ones. You may want to spend every waking moment searching for answers, but they cannot always keep up with your excitement. So be careful not to overload them. Sometimes it's best to let them set the pace when it comes to how quickly they need to know things. Some abductees find it is best not to talk about something until asked about it by their spouse.

9. "What I tell my support people will upset or hurt them."

It is true that many of the things you have to talk about will upset those around you, particularly if you don't have the smoothest of relationships with your spouse. But no matter what, don't lie to your support people. Sometimes it's so hard to look at your support people and tell them something that you know will hurt them. If you are going to tell them, however, commit yourself to telling them the truth, no matter what. If you start lying, they won't know what to think when they find out the truth—and eventually, they will. Furthermore, using the truth to guide what you say is much easier than trying to remember which partial truths you have said to whom.

Often lies start when we soften the corners of an event to make it easier for our loved ones to accept it. We may tell them that we were given a physical exam, but we don't mention the fetal (or sperm) extraction because we know that will upset them. Be careful of this type of thing. Someday you will grow beyond the ability and need for lies, and when the truth does come out, you may find that you have blown away your support people.

chapter seven

Controlling the Fear

The best way to control your fear is to understand it. You have to face it and acknowledge it. Here are some easy and effective steps to help you do this:

1. Keep writing in your journal.

Just like with cycles, one of the best ways to get a handle on your fear and what is happening to you is to keep a diary. Write down all you can remember about your experiences and what you feel about them. This gives you a reference you can always go back to if you feel you need to remind yourself of times past. Many times it's good to look back and see how far you have come. Again, you don't have to use terms like "ETs" or "aliens." If you are afraid someone will find your journal and use it against you in some way, use code words or write your experiences in the form of science fiction or fantasy. Only you need to know that the story is nonfiction and the hero of the story is you!

2. Keep a record of your levels of fear and anxiety.

It's important to make some kind of record and chart your day-to-day fears and anxieties on a scale of 0 to 10. You can do this easily by marking the level of fear you are experiencing from day to day on a calendar that has room to write on. If you are feeling relaxed and calm, chart your day as a 0. If you are a little apprehensive, you may want to put down a 2 or 3. Nervousness should be marked down as a higher number—say a 5, and a 7 or 8 would indicate that you are downright frightened.

Be honest with yourself, especially if you are making little notes on the calendar beside the numbers. I found it helpful to jot down anything I knew that triggered my tension (TV shows, strange lights or sounds, odd dreams, familiar smells, etc.).

Don't pull off the pages of your calendar and toss them out at the end of the month. Keep them and study them from time to time. You may find a pattern forming in the cycle of your fears. This pattern may even become predictable. Then you can learn to anticipate when to expect periods of less nervousness and try to let yourself relax during those times.

Teaching yourself to relax during quiet times will let you rebuild your strength, so that your tense times are less stressful on you.

3. Practice talking to the ETs.

You should resolve to talk to the ETs and practice doing so. Then you will be able to talk to them when you would otherwise be speechless with fear. (I know that you may think that this is a little strange, but believe me, it works.)

Tell them what you want and expect from them. If you tell them you want to remember more, you may find the next day that you do. If you say you are remembering too much and it scares you, they may make an effort to help you forget. (Before you ask them to do this, think carefully. You will be quite upset if you wake one morning and everything you've been working so hard to know is only a vague hazy memory.) Don't bother telling them to leave you alone and never come back. You know they won't. Besides, if you open a dialogue with them, why waste it? Use it to better understand what is happening.

4. Do not react violently.

You must avoid reacting to fear with violence.

My husband is a very loving and gentle man, but like any man in his situation, he was feeling confused, threatened and scared. He was being told that aliens were coming into his house at night and taking half his family away. How else could he feel, but completely helpless and violated? To protect his family, he began to sleep with a 2x4 beside the bed. He kept his hand on it at all times. He said that the next time an alien came near us, he would lob its head off.

I knew this was useless. I think he did, too, but he was doing what he could understand. I could not persuade him to get rid of the board— until one night, that board almost turned into tragedy.

At about 3:00 in the morning, my husband heard someone walk into our bedroom. All he could see in the dark was a three-and-a-half foot form approaching the bed. His hand gripped the board, and he was ready to swing it when my four-year-old daughter whined out, "Daddy, I can't sleep."

He dropped the board and grabbed our little girl in his arms. I could see his eyes welling up. He knew what had almost happened. When everything calmed down, I put our little one back to bed. While I did, he went downstairs and tossed the board into the basement.

My husband does not like for me to tell that story, but I think it's important. The point of the story is clear. The ETs paralyze you when they come into your home so you won't do something like that to them. If you can swing that board or fire that gun, you are only going to hurt someone you love very much. What a tragedy that would be!

Figure 7. Hetar sitting.

The best way to cope with fear is to go forward and discover all you can about yourself and your experiences. Find others you feel at home with and spend time with them when you can. As you read on, you will find more ways to take control of your situation and that, too, will help you control the fear. Remember, you're not completely help-less.

When we are children, we fear many things—the dark, monsters in the closet, thunder. When we are older, we don't. Why? Because we *grow* out of those fears. So, once again, growing is the key.

chapter eight

Seeking Friends

In chapter six, I said you need not shout from the highest mountain about your experiences, but in no way do I mean you shouldn't tell anyone. In fact, you are going to have to tell someone. If you don't, you'll go nuts. I find that abductees who experience cycles often think in circles, especially if they are left alone for a long time. Often, experiencers have to air their thoughts to someone else in order to understand the totality of what they are thinking about. Having a friend to talk to is very helpful. You can tell a good friend anything and not be judged.

Even with a good, supportive network of non-abductee friends, you won't feel complete. Remember, we are community-oriented beings, and we have gone through extensive training and bonding in community units. We need each other to survive, and once you become aware that you are an experiencer, you need to seek out others of your own kind.

As you feel stronger self-confidence surrounding your experiences, seek out positive people like yourself. If you are still going through the fear, talk to others who lived through it already and seem to have a handle on it. See how they cope. Talk to others who are also afraid. You will be very relieved to know that you are not the only one. Under these kinds of conditions, you could build some strong friendships.

As you progress and grow, keep seeking out others around you who are growing. Always keep in mind that, if it doesn't feel like home, it isn't right for you. Eventually you will connect with someone (or some group) with whom you feel comfortable.

I wish I could tell you exactly whom you should call to make these connections, but I cannot. I can't even give you names and numbers of individual experiencers. Because of the personal nature of this type of experience, most people don't want their names given out without good cause. Many will not release their names at all. Still there are many ways to find others like you. Here are some suggestions:

1. Try finding a local UFO-research group.

One place you could start would be your local branch of MUFON (Mutual UFO Network) or another such UFO-research group. Many experiencers I know started meeting people this way. (See appendix three for a list of support resources.) If you are unable to find a number in your telephone directory, ask the reference librarian at your local library for help. If no local organization can be found, ask for a listing of national organizations and their addresses and phone numbers. If the organization you chose has a local chapter, the national office can direct you to it.

2. Check out a New Age book store.

New Age bookstores usually sell books about UFOs and related subjects. Many experiencers frequent them. If you ask around, you will probably find someone who knows something. The person-to-person route is often the best. I recommend that you contact a real flesh-and-blood experiencer and talk to her. You need more than just the printed form letter that you might get from some of the bigger national organizations.

3. Attend lectures and conferences.

Watch the newspapers for lectures on UFOs. Many times the speaker (or even other abductees in the audience) can direct you to a good local group. You may be surprised, but it is not uncommon for experiencers to attend a conference or lecture and recognize others in the crowd that they have never met before (at least not on Earth). It's a great way to meet people.

No matter what route you take, be careful of people who only want to collect your experiences and move on. Be particularly wary of anyone who is quick to suggest hypnosis without first telling you all the other options and possible side effects, or who will not commit to providing you some support after hypnosis. Trust me, hypnosis is no picnic.

You also should make sure that you are not just being studied (unless you have agreed to it beforehand). It may be exciting to be the center of attention for a while, but when you realize that someone else just "raped" you of your experiences for their upcoming book or lecture tour, you feel pretty let down and hurt. Besides, you need to be nurtured and fed, not dissected and studied. Not all people out there lecturing and writing books is this type of leech. Actually, very few are. But don't take that chance until you have all the facts.

So take your time and seek out others who have had abduction experiences—people that you can bond with. You can nurture each other. Make sure that you do find others of similar experience. If you are an advanced part of the Gemini community, you may find that quick in/ quick outs are unable to sympathize with or understand all you feel about your experiences. If, on the other hand, you are a quick in/quick out, you may not be ready to hear what is said when a group of Gemini people with clear memories get together.

Similar Events

Once you contact other experiencers and get involved with a support group, you will be exposed to many stories of others' abduction events. Sometimes they will seem very strange and foreign to you. But more often, you will find people talking about things that sound so familiar that you may wonder if they happened to you, too. It's a very strange feeling to wonder whether something has happened to you, or you are just imagining it.

You see, more often than not, once an experiencer begins to talk to other experiencers, memories that have been buried away in the subconscious will be triggered.

Because many of us have had very similar experiences, when someone else talks about what is happening to him, he is bound to come upon something he remembers that happened to you, too. To make matters more complicated, many times experiencers do not recognize the similarity of the event until some time later, when they are quiet and alone.

I cannot begin to tell you how many people have talked to me about this type of thing. One woman called me up to ask, "Am I crazy?" After I had told a group about an event that had happened to me, she had gone home and dreamed the whole event over again with her as the subject of the test. She really believed she was only reliving what I said, rather than having a personal experience.

I asked her about the dream, and we talked awhile. Before long, she and I both realized that she was telling me things about the test that I did not talk about in the support group. She actually cleared up some things that I was having a hard time defining about the event. Also, there were small differences between her "dream" and my event. It was obvious that she had experienced the same test I had, and that my talking about it had triggered a memory in her, not a fantasy.

I truly cannot say that whenever you hear an abduction story that triggers something in you, you are remembering something that really happened to you and you are not just sympathizing with the teller. We are all empathic and can easily absorb the feelings of others. But it appears we usually don't. If we did, abductees would think every experience other abductees have is familiar to them. But that's just not true.

The fact is, once you hear of an event that's familiar to you, you are bound to fill in the blanks of your own experience. Doing so can fill you with a mixture of confusion and self-doubt. You may begin to doubt that you are remembering something that truly happened. You may begin to think that you are only making yourself believe the event happened to you. Then comes the next step down the ladder of self-doubt. You begin to wonder if you have any valid memories at all, no matter how vivid the memories. This self-doubt really hurts your feelings of validation, especially if anyone around you is saying things like, "It's all in your head," or "You watch too much TV."

Once again, I urge you to use your heart—not your head—in these matters. If you believe something happened to you, it did. If someone tells you that something happened to you, but you really felt as if it didn't, then it didn't.

Remember the concepts of perception and subjective reality. We react to the experiences that we believe we have lived through. Only you know what happened or did not happen to you. Don't doubt yourself when you react to an event that someone else talks about. If it happened to you too, your subconscious mind knows it and may react to it. These reactions may be as simple as an edgy feeling or a cloudy memory, or as vivid as a realistic dream or a feeling of panic.

Whatever the reaction, realize that you have a *right* to react. You are neither going crazy nor being oversensitive. You are simply experiencing something that you were not previously fully aware of. Keep that in mind when someone tells you an experience that seems to set you on edge and causes you to awaken the next morning with a memory of the event happening to you. Just because it happened to someone else and they remembered it consciously before you did, does not mean he has a patent on it, or owns the experience. Just because someone else talks about it first, doesn't mean it didn't happen to you as well.

Owning an Event

Some experiencers believe that any event they talk about first belongs to them. They are quick to accuse others of "stealing" their experiences. I even heard of one experiencer threatening to sue another because she wrote an article about an event that was similar to something that happened to the first.

The fact is that hundreds, possibly thousands, of abductees get the same messages and visions from the ETs at any given time. It will amaze you at first, how often you will wake up with a concept or memory about your experiences, call another abductee, and find out she woke up with the same exact concept or memory.

Unfortunately, some experiencers feel that they have a kind of copyright on the things that happen to them, even if they happen to others, too. They believe that other experiencers will "steal" their "ideas" in order to either get rich or to get attention from a researcher or doctor. (Actually, no one can steal your "idea," because the abduction event was not your idea in the first place.)

Part of this problem goes back to humankind's greatest weakness: *ego.* The idea that if something happened to you, you own it and it can never happen to anyone else is just another way of your ego saying, "I'm afraid of what's happening to me, and I can't cope with it. Other people around me seem to be able to cope with it. Therefore, I've decided that my experiences are so much more complex and intense than those of anyone around me that they could only happen to me and me alone."

When someone comes along who threatens a person's ego reasoning by saying he shared a similar experience, the person feels threatened. In order to protect the safe little world she created for her ego, she may accuse the "interloper" of pilfering the event. She may even be quick to express her doubts about the validity of any of the other's abductions.

I have to admit, a person is bound to feel uneasy once in a while if others continually tell her of experiences that are just like hers. This is particularly true if the same person comes to her every time she talks. But there is no reason to be upset by this.

It really is not that unusual. Often, experiencers in a group who are unsure of themselves or shy about their experiences may feel you would understand how they feel because you have a lot of events in common, so they come to you with all that they remember.

More often than not, you may feel excited when you talk to someone who shares an event with you. Talking about your experiences with someone who shares them can bring about a feeling of freedom and relief such as you have never experienced before. A good, supportive environment of experiencers provides a sense of community. After all, we are all part of the greater community we share with the ETs. Still—and I cannot stress this enough—if you don't feel you belong in a group you are involved with, then you don't. *Just leave.*

Keep your chin up; you do belong somewhere, and you will find out where. You may even find it in the first place you look. Many people do.

chapter nine

Procedures and Tests

In this chapter, I will discuss some of the medical and psychological procedures that many of us go through when we are with the ETs. Some of them may make you uneasy. About one-third of the experiencers with whom I have shared this material have felt uneasy reading about the procedures.

The procedures I describe are far from the only things done to abductees. They may differ in your memory due to many factors, including (but not limited to) perception. If you don't understand what I mean by perception, you can try this little test at home:

Invite some friends over to your house. Make sure they don't know what you plan to do. Arrange ahead of time for someone who is a stranger to your friends to run through the room, carrying something small in his hands (or to run through the room, grab something from a table) and run out. Then ask your friends to describe the runner. What color was his hair? What did his clothes look like? What was the runner carrying (or what did he take)? Many times, the gist of what we abductees experience is very much the same—yet each may report details differently, according to his own perception.

Control Wands

Many procedures involve different kinds of sticks or wands. (See Figure 8.) These wands are used by the ETs to control things like pain and pleasure.

One of the two most common types of wands appears to be a simple silver/white shaft about ten inches long that is tapered at one end. This regular type of wand is used most often by the ETs themselves. It can induce searing pain at just a touch, particularly if the touch is to a temple, wrist or ankle. It can also induce intense pleasure. Often, if touched with a wand on the forehead, a subject will experience a fantasy of pleasure or even an orgasm. The ETs also use these wands to block pain.

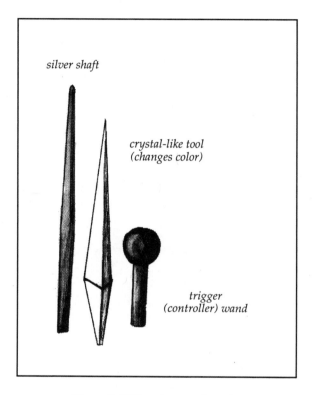

silver shaft

crystal-like tool
(changes color)

trigger
(controller) wand

Figure 8. Different types of wands.

The other type of commonly used wand is a short silver shaft with a ball on the top. These are used most often by small greys or controller/empaths. They can deliver a stunning shock that immobilizes the target. These wands work on a trigger system, much like a gun, or by touching the subject with the balled end.

All the other wands I know of use the channeling of thought as their primary trigger.

Common Physical Procedures

Sperm extraction

The most common procedure that people seem to remember and describe to me deals with the ETs' breeding program. Men describe a procedure during which they are placed on a table and a tube, which comes from the wall, is placed over the penis. Some also remember having another tube inserted into the rectum (this is probably to stimulate the prostate gland). In a second or so, the men experience a strange sort of orgasm (many say it is without pleasure), and the sperm is forcibly collected. Some men have told me that they thought they were having exciting dreams, only to awake and find themselves on the table. More feel that this is because during the beginning of the procedure, they were still "turned off," and were dreaming.

Some men experience sperm extraction as a kind of rape. They are on their backs and a female ET straddles them until they ejaculate. Often at this point, the female ET seems to disappear, leaving them on the table with the tube on the penis.

Implantation and extraction of fetuses

Women undergo a more complex series of procedures. A woman is put on the table, and her legs are guided apart and placed along the sides of the table. (See Figure 9.) Sometimes a woman will remember stirrups like those on a gynecologists' examination table. A tube that comes out of the wall is inserted into her body vaginally and eggs are taken from her.

In much the same fashion, the ETs can insert genetic material into a woman's uterus. Usually, after this is done, the woman is told that she is now pregnant. Some women have told me that they remember extreme pressure on the lower body during this procedure. Some have even been made to have an orgasm at this time. This is not done by clitoral stimulation, but rather when the tall gray being touches them on the forehead with his longest finger or with a wand.

Several months later—usually not more that two or three—the fetal implant is removed. This is usually done through "phasing." Phasing is a way to make one object pass through another. The fetus is removed with very little or no pain, and is taken away, usually with the placenta intact.

Most women think the fetuses look very well-developed for how long they gestated. Small greys usually take the fetus away by means of levitation. Only one woman I spoke to remembers any kind of contractions like normal labor.

Figure 9. Woman being examined by greys.

At this time, some women are implanted with additional genetic material. Some are not. Some of the women I've spoke to remember screaming out during the procedure. Some feel it was from pain. Others think it was from fear. Some even found that they were crying to see the child before it was taken away. Personally, I do not remember any pain during these procedures, but I know that whenever I am in pain, Hetar can touch me and I feel nothing.

Each time a fetus has been removed from me, Hetar (who always stands at my left side, holding my hand) has thanked me for another strong son or daughter. He says I have 63 children to date (not counting the three I have on Earth and the two I carried for Hetar that were created from my mother's genetic material). Honestly, I cannot say that I remember having that many.

Probe and sensor implantation

Another common procedure is the insertion of a small sensor into the forward part of the brain by way of the nose. Hetar said these sensors are for our protection. I'm not too sure what he means by that, but he does not care to explain further.

Some other common points of insertion are the back of the head, where the skull and spine meet, through the ears, and just behind the ears. Many people have also had things put in their forearms and wrists.

The insertion of these instruments may cause a little bleeding or a small white scar at the insertion point. Sometimes a small, hard, BB-like thing can be felt under the skin. A few experiencers I know even remember sneezing hard and having a small metal ball fall out of their noses. One person told me that the ball dissolved before she could give it to anyone.

System flushing

Another procedure that many people remember (and, in fact, go through on a regular basis) is the flushing of the digestive system. The ETs put tubes in the throat, urethra and/or anus, and pump liquid through them in much the same way we might flush out an automobile's radiator.

This is not a very pleasant experience. It always makes me feel as if I am choking.

The last time I knew this was going to happen to me, I complained feverishly. Hetar looked at me and said that if I don't want this to happen so often, I should stop eating so much red meat. Then he touched me on the forehead and I fell asleep. I don't remember the procedure, and I am glad of that.

Examination and removal of body parts

At times, the ETs may cut open your arms or even take your organs out to examine them in detail. During these operations there is not much bleeding, if any at all. This fact usually surprises experiencers when they first remember it.

Often, if you ask the ETs why they are doing these things to you, they will explain that they are adapting or amending your body so that you will be better able to do your part in the job given you. Is this true? You'll have to decide that for yourself. I believe it is. But it is one of the things that people never seem to believe, no matter what other Geminis tell them—until they experience it themselves.

How is it that the ETs can cut us wide open, and maybe even take out major organs, without killing us? Hetar told me that they can do these things because they have control over time. In these events, they are utilizing time in a nonlinear fashion. (Just a note about time: Time is a dimension, like length, width and height. As humans, we can move through the length, width and height at will, yet we can only move in one direction in time. The ETs seem to be able to slow down, speed up and otherwise manipulate time.)

I was told that occasionally they only make us think we are being disassembled, and at other times, they really do it. The trick is to know one from the other. Or does it really make a difference? If you truly believe you are being taken apart, then in that frame of reality, you really are.

Common Mental Procedures

Another category of procedures is what I call "head-game" tests, or perception/reaction tests. These encompass all the double speak and unanswered questions, as well as those strange little episodes that abductees are subjected to that seem to have no reason at all, except to frustrate and confuse us. The following are some examples of the most common head games ETs play.

1. The old "give-them-proof" game

In this type of event, the ETs offer definite proof of their existence—proof that could be taken to the people on Earth—only to take it back at the last minute.

A friend of mine was with his own counterpart to my Hetar. His mentor said to him, "It must be very hard for you to go home and not have any proof of your work here with me. So I have decided you can take this book home with you." He handed him a book that contained writing and pictures of the greys' world. The man told me he was very excited and held the book with his eyes opened wide. His mentor led him to the gray spot on the floor to send him home. Just as he was about to leave, his mentor took the book away and said, "I'm sorry; I made a mistake. You can't have that book."

2. The "give-you-something-you-want" game

Along the same theme as the proof game is the game of giving someone something they desperately want, only to take it away.

A good example of this happened in my life several years ago. My husband and I were trying very hard to have a baby. We had been seeing a fertility specialist. My desire to have a baby was overpowering. The ETs used my desire to play a mind game on me.

Hetar led me to a room and handed me a small baby that looked very human. He said it was not fair that I was not able to have a baby of my own. Then he told me that he was giving me that baby. He said it was mine and I could keep it. I asked him what he meant by, "You can keep it." He said I could take it home with me. I asked him what I would say to my friends and family to explain the baby. He said I didn't even have to worry about that. He would take care of everything. I believed he had the ability to do something like that, so I believed him when he said I could keep it. Hetar then left the room and left me alone with the little infant. I cuddled it and got very attached to it in a short time. I even named it. Then, after I was completely attached to the child, he came back in and said, "I'm sorry; I made a mistake. The father of this child has red hair. Your husband does not. I can't let you take this infant."

I felt as if my insides had just been ripped apart, and I started to cry. Hetar just stood in front of me and said nothing, as a little grey came in and took the baby away from me.

Both examples illustrate the frustration circles the ETs sometimes put you in. Are they trying to get reactions from you? Are they trying to break your spirit?

I often ask Hetar what the mind games are for, but I never really get a complete answer. Once he said, "You must recognize deception when you experience it." I usually get answers like, "You ask things you already know," or "You already have that answer." Those types of replies can be more frustrating than the game itself.

3. The "choosing" game

Almost every experiencer I talk to about abductions has had this, or something extremely similar, done to them:

The abductee is led into a room full of babies or small children. The ET who is with her tells her one child is hers. (Sometimes he tells her several are hers.) The rest of them are from other people. She is then asked to look at the children and choose which one is hers. Sometimes the ETs even ask her to smell children to see if she can pick out her child that way.

It seems that they have been doing this test to hundreds, perhaps thousands, of abductees for quite some time. Are they really trying to see if humans can pick out their own young from a large group? If that were the only purpose for this test, wouldn't they have found their answer already?

Not long ago, I was subjected to another test that seemed useless. I was led into a room. Along the wall were three men. I recognized all three. I had worked with all of them in the past. The same small greys led in three little boys about five years old and placed the boys between me and the men—one boy in front of each man. Then, Hetar said, "These are yours." He pointed to the children. "This man is this one's father," he said, as he motioned to the man and the boy in front of him. "This man is this one's father." He motioned to the next pair. "This man is this one's father." He motioned to the third pair.

I have no idea if these children were really created by Hetar using genetic material taken from these three men and me.

"Which child do you love the best?" Hetar asked. I assume that he wanted me to choose a child based on what I knew of their fathers, as I had never seen any of the children before.

"I don't know them," I replied. "I can't choose."

"What shall I do with these children?" he asked in a strange tone of voice.

I shrugged. "Bring them back where they were, I guess."

Hetar nodded and the children were led away. When I walked out of the room, the men were still standing there. What was the purpose? If you know, please tell me. (My address is available in appendix three.)

4. Reaction tests

Reaction tests are far more complicated to explain. These tests cause many problems and memory blocks. Reaction tests are by far the most emotionally upsetting and hardest to absorb meaning from. Often when a person panics and has to be controlled by an empath, it's because of a reaction test, rather than a medical test.

The range of intensity a person can experience can be anything from a vision that makes him melancholy to making him live out a scenario that terrifies him beyond compare. While exploring these visions, most people discover a strong spiritual side to these tests. This is because many of the visions revolve around a "New World Order" theme. (This idea differs from George Bush's concept of the same name.)

Quite a few people, after exploring these visions, find that many of their childhood fears and recurrent nightmares stem from what they experience during these events.

Another thing these visions tend to create in experiencers is what I call the "be-prepared" reaction. Experiencers usually share certain strange quirks that have surprised some non-abductee researchers with their regularity. The "be-prepared" reaction is one of these quirks.

One example of a common be-prepared reaction is the way experiencers tend to check for exits when they enter a strange place. Another is the way we look for safe places as shelter in case we cannot get out. If you do these things, you may not even realize it because they stem from habit, rather that from fear or panic.

One of my experiencer friends told me she did not like working in her new office because she was far away from the door and there was no direct route to it. Her fear was not strong enough to stop her from working, but it did bother her once in a while. It confused her because she had no desire to run out of the door. She just wanted to know that she could if she had to.

Another man I know said he heard a loud bang and had to fight a compulsion to get under his desk. A large box had fallen on the floor above him. When I asked him what he had thought the bang was, he said, "I thought they blew it all up."

Many abductees have very definite fears about nuclear war or the world blowing up. My mother and grandmother had such fears. Once, when I was a child, a gas leak caused a store near my grandmother's house to explode in the middle of the night.

My grandmother, awakened by the explosion and hearing windows of her own house breaking, telephoned my mother in a panic.

"It's the end of the world!" she screamed into the receiver. Then she began to bark out commands for my mother to get to the basement. My mother also panicked. She was ready to rush us all into the basement to hide from fallout. My father, who to my knowledge is not an experiencer, pointed out the fact that if an H-bomb had just blown up over the city, not only would the phones be out, but there wouldn't be anyone alive to answer them.

As a result of these reaction visions, we share a deep, strong survival instinct. Some experiencers even remember being told that they have to be smart and save themselves "from the explosion and the flash-over." They are told, "We [ETs] can handle the radiation, but if your body is a pile of ashes, forget it."

Many abductees remember being made to practice surviving nuclear wars during reaction tests. They are made to believe a nuclear explosion had just happened and they have to get to shelter or die. The experience is very real and very upsetting. When you are living through it, you may not know it's only a test.

I am not saying that the world is heading for a nuclear war, only that we experiencers are being conditioned for one.

During reaction tests, people are usually unable to move and are made to experience visions that provoke severe reaction. Often, after a vision has ended, the grey will ask, "Do you understand?" If you say no, you may have to experience it again. Then, when it's over again, the ET will ask, "Do you understand?" If you answer yes, the session may be over. But if you answer yes just to stop the visions, make it convincing. If you are lying, they will usually know it and make you see the visions again.

The point to some of these visions is clear. For others, it is not clear at all. Yet the ETs will still ask, "Do you understand?" For example, Hetar showed me a vision of my little daughter sitting in a field of yellow grass. Suddenly, she stood up, screamed and ran away. As she was running, her body appeared to fall apart. Her arms and legs and head fall to the ground around her lifeless torso. Oddly enough, I knew the vision was not a threat, though it seemed like one. When it ended and he asked, "Do you understand?" I had to say no. Even today, almost ten years later, I am not sure what the point was.

Some people have theorized that the ETs are making us live through these extremes of emotion so that they can collect the enzymes and chemicals given off by our brains at these times and use them to experience emotions. They base this theory on the mistaken belief that the ETs have no emotions of their own, and therefore have to use us to simulate them for their own use.

Nothing could be further from the truth. Although the ETs I have encountered sometimes express their emotions quite differently from the way we do, they are very emotional. And they have a very bizarre sense of humor. Have you ever awakened with your head in your pillow case? They think that's a riot. Another favorite trick of theirs is tucking you into your bed so tightly that you can barely breathe.

With all this in mind, I cannot believe that the collection of enzymes to simulate emotions is the reason they perform reaction tests on us. Instead, I think they are teaching us things we must know and understand in order to grow. I base my opinion on something Hetar said to me. He said, "All experiences, no matter if you think them good or bad, feed you and make you strong." He also said, "Experience this that is life, so you can touch eternity."

Still, some of the things that ETs show experiencers just don't make sense to us here on Earth. But, I wonder…do they perhaps make sense to that part of us that is more than just a physical body living on terra firma?

5. *Practice visions*

Some of the visions that you may experience will not be reaction tests. You may be made to experience a vision to provide yourself with a controlled environment in order to practice the skills of your particular job. For example, if you are an empath who hasn't really worked with anyone who is considered dangerous, the ETs might arrange a practice vision for you, in which you will think you are working as an empath approaching a dangerous individual. Then they can see how well you will do before they actually take the chance of exposing you to real danger.

I have been made to practice one particular vision again and again on many occasions. I experience a scene of global destruction. It is horrible. As people are panicking and dying around me, my mind floats into the air (or perhaps into a different dimension or an out-of-body state). As the people die and are transformed to beings of light, the darkness of their pain and fear comes away from them and remains behind. It is dangerous. It can return to the world and destroy everything left. It appears to me as a thick, black, liquid evil. It is an overpowering mass of darkness that is spreading over me. I'm somehow blocking it from spreading over the world. I am drawing it away from the earth's surface like a sponge drawing water.

All the while, I hear Hetar's voice. He is ordering me to consume it—to eat it and digest it. I know I have to do it, but it is going to be the worst pain, the greatest soul ache, that I will ever experience. I know this, but I have to do it. There is so much thick dark for me to swallow! (This "swallowing" is more symbolism. The act is one of the soul, not one of a physical nature. When I absorb the darkness, I don't actually chew and swallow it.) The black is choking me, making me writhe with pain and gasp for breath.

"Do it. You must," Hetar urges.

So I do it. I have to. (Sometimes I try to fight it, but eventually I have to give in.) The darkness passes through me. I experience all the cold evil in it as it passes. I digest it into an inert form. (If you can do this, you know what I mean; otherwise, the only way I can describe it is, it's like turning the liquid color into a solid color that can no longer spread or hurt anything. The actions that cause the liquid to become solid were taught to me through the use of symbols. So, what exactly happens when I "digest" the darkness is, in my mind, symbolic of eating and excreting waste.) The pain that comes from the total void of love and light in the darkness is beyond my ability to describe. Even as I write this, I feel a little shaky thinking about it.

When I feel like I've taken as much as I possibly can and the black viscous liquid is overpowering me, Hetar insists that I eat more—that I eat it all. Finally, when there is no more black, dark evil, I fall down, exhausted and panting. Hetar is at my side. He strokes my forehead and tells me that I'm a good girl. As he touches me, the memory of the dark pain fades, and is replaced by the violet light that I usually see in my soul.

Hetar tells me, time and time again, that he is making me practice for what I will someday have to do. As you can see, it is not the type of thing one has an opportunity to practice in "real life" until it happens (if it ever will happen). So the visions are the only way I have to practice the skills I must develop to do it.

6. The "let's-see" method

Sometimes the ETs may put you together with another abductee and just watch to see what you two will do together. Sometimes they may set up a situation. They may give you an object or task. At other times, they say and do nothing.

One such test proved to be a little embarrassing for me. Hetar asked me to look at several men he had assembled in a room. He asked me to choose which man I thought was the most attractive sexually. Next, I was put in a room with the man I had chosen. Hetar and others were watching, I'm sure. The man and I just chatted a little. He was very nervous and I was more than a little uncomfortable, because I just picked him out of a sex-appeal lineup, and he knew it.

After a while, Hetar came in and took me away. He asked me why I did not have sex with the man I had found attractive. I cannot recall my exact answer, but I'm sure it wasn't what he expected!

7. When you are the equipment

During another type of test, you may be asked to hold something being used on someone else, or you may even be asked to let the ETs use your body to test out someone else.

For example, once I was asked to help out with a test on a halfling. I was given only a vague explanation of what was to happen. I did not volunteer for this, but I knew I had no choice, so I was resigned to doing it. I was not pleased, but I didn't fight it. Instead, I just chose to ignore it.

It seems the ETs needed to test a halfling man to see if he could have intercourse normally. It appears that sexual dysfunction is a definite problem for a high percentage of halflings. In order to test this particular halfling, I was put on a table with my legs hanging off the end. I couldn't move. The halfling entered the room. He was thin, about 5'4" tall, and had sparse, light hair and crooked, irregular teeth. He had wide eyes that resembled a Japanese cartoon character. He came up to me, entered me and did his thing. It was only a matter of minutes. He spoke no words and walked away.

As soon as he was gone, two small greys came in and put a white instrument in me to collect what the halfling had just put there.

When I related this event to a friend, she asked if I felt raped. Oddly enough, I didn't. It was not an act of violence. It was just another medical procedure. This time I was the equipment.

What I did feel was used.

There are other times when sex is used by the ET as a control tool or a tool of domination, especially with difficult men. The idea is to put the subject in a submissive position. A female ET will straddle the man and keep him helpless in her control. Even though the man usually is feeling pleasure (a lot of men will not accept this at first, but most discover it is true), he is well aware that he is being totally dominated by the ET. She will stare at him intensely. When the idea of submission is clear to the man, the woman will allow the act to come to its end and quietly leave. It is very unsettling to the man. That's the point.

Although this sounds the same as the sperm-gathering procedure, those who have experienced both tell me it is very different. The gathering procedure does not include the forceful message of dominance and submission of the latter event. Also, during the submission procedure, the female ET does not disappear, leaving the man with a hose on his genitals.

Some female controller/empaths have seen themselves in ET form, performing this procedure on human men. Women often describe what is happening as a form of bonding, rather than of dominance.

These things can all sound confusing, but it is important not to confuse acts of domination with acts of bonding. They are very different, and most Geminis know them both.

People often ask me how I could have such a positive attitude about the ETs when they have done these strange things to me. I take everything that scares me or confuses me with a grain of salt. You see, as I travel down my own personal road of discovery, I find that things that confused or frightened me in the past are now clear and make sense. I trust in my heart, and it tells me that I am in no danger. I trust in my mentor, Hetar, when he tells me that as I grow, so will my ability to see the order of the universe. I know that things I cannot understand today will be clear eventually. So I cope with them and store them away until a time comes when I can put them in order and make sense of them.

One last note about the physical test and procedures. It seems to be a pattern that the more one does in the Gemini community, the more responsibility he takes, the more he learns and understands, and the fewer physical procedures he is exposed to.

chapter ten

The Spiritual Side

What's going on? What's this spiritual stuff? To explore this, you have to explore yourself. I hate to sound like I'm "copping out," but you do have all the answers in you—and your own answers are the only ones that will perfectly satisfy your questions.

It is no secret that the ETs are creating a race of halflings. But why? To explore this question, we have to dig into the nonphysical side of this experience.

The ETs are telling us that the world is going through some dramatic changes and will soon "end" as we know it. But it will not end completely. There will be people who survive past this "end" and make a new life on a new Earth. They call this a "New World Order."

People have been saying this for thousands of years. The earliest record of it that comes to my mind was written on an obelisk from the time of Hammurabi (circa 1900-1600 B.C.). (This is a little factoid that I pick up from my grammar school days.) It said that the gods would return and the world would end in the early part of the twenty-first century (based on modern interpretation of the calendar of the day).

Even 100 years ago, just before the turn of this century, there was a movement much like today's New Age movement. Many people believed the world was going to end. They believed it was then going to go through a reorganization for those who lived through the final days. All of this was supposed to happen at the turn of the century, almost a hundred years ago. It did not end, but shifted into a new reality that would have been inconceivable for those living in the 1890s.

Another theme the ETs talk about consistently is the "caring-for-the-earth" theme. They continually make us aware of the pain we are putting the living Mother Earth through.

They also tell us that the Earth is in a dampening field that prevents the people from discovering their full potential. They say that soon the Earth will pass out of this field, allowing the mass population to become aware and awake to all the worlds beyond the physical one of the five senses. Everyone will develop new psychic skills and energy—not just good people, but bad people and everyone in between. The cunning and the wicked will exploit these changes to cause trouble.

But this is only going to be part of the danger. As the people become more aware, they will begin to grow, and they will need teachers. Eventually they will let go of their inner darkness. Some of us experiencers will work with the population to help them release the darkness (just as the empaths do on the ships). I and others like me will be working to digest this darkness and make it inert so it will never come back to Earth and destroy the people (see the practice visions described in chapter nine).

The abductees will take over positions of teachers and caretakers of the populations. Then, when things settle down, the ETs will introduce their halflings to the Earth to live with us and continue the greys' genetic line. They also say that this new world will be one of peace, art and unconditional love.

But before all this is supposed to happen, it seems that there are going to be some events of great havoc, such as major earthquakes, fires, tidal waves, etc. The greys say these events will be global in proportion.

It's really quite upsetting if true. The greys assure us, time and time again, that it is. On more than one occasion they alluded to the fact that they will have something to do with starting these changes. When I asked Hetar if they will have anything to do with the predicted disasters, he said, "Not at all. The changes are coming because the Earth is sick of the pain humans are putting her through."

Other statements have led me to believe that they may intend to have their halfling race replace the human race, and that the replacement may be effected by crossbreeding until the two races are indistinguishable from one another. Some people believe that this process is already underway. They contend that we experiencers are not quite human because we are the next generation in their development of this race. Our children will be the next and so on. (I wonder if this is why my daughter has 13 complete sets of ribs?)

A few people have told me that they think the greys are going to replace the human race completely in one major event, but that seems improbable. If they wanted to force the human race into submission, or simply destroy it, they could have done so years ago. I know that there are some greys (but not many) who still seem to see humans as animals, or a lower form of life.

The idea that we abductees are being prepared for the end of the world is not hard to fathom when you think of the reaction tests. Is it really going to end? Abductees cannot agree. Some believe it will happen no matter what. Others believe prayers can put it off. Still others believe it's just a residual effect from the visions we are subjected to. Many people even believe it is just a cruel kind of mental experiment that they are conducting on us—their subjects.

The question of the spiritual side is complex. Some of the earliest abduction reports contain no real talk about spiritual things (experiencing past or future lives or the vastness of eternity, seeing angels, receiving messages from a Godlike force, etc.). It seems odd that although these earlier experiencers had quite similar physical experiences, they did not report any visions of angels or the like. Even though they experienced very similar reaction tests, they did not report the connection to "prophecy" that the new generation of abductees experience.

This could be explained by one big difference between the encounters described by the new generation of experiencers and the older one. People who have been experiencing things during the last generation have reported being subjected to more radical physical procedures than those reported a generation before them.

The previous generation of abductees experienced the breeding procedures, some simple physical test, and perhaps some simple reaction tests done to them, but little more than that.

Today, experiencers undergo physical examinations that would normally kill them had they been done on Earth. Gemini people and even quick in/quick outs routinely remember having major organs removed or having their bodies totally cut in half. This is done to the person in a "time stop" situation, so that their bodies do not degenerate and die. They seldom even bleed.

Often, the spiritual side of the experience happens during these radical tests. Could it be that the subjects are having near-death experiences? While under such stressful situations, they often see the tunnel that leads to the white light reported by people who die on operating tables in Earth hospitals and are subsequently resuscitated. They may even see dead relatives. Frequently they find themselves floating in a cloudy void, where they begin to see visions of their lives and their role in the universe.

Is it real or just a side effect of the ETs' work? The people who are worked on in this way come back with a heightened psychic sense. The more they are worked on, the more the sense sharpens. (This also happens after a near-death experience.)

During one experience, my body was taken apart. I slipped into a vision. In this vision, I was flying in a cloudy void. I was drifting. I felt very warm and comfortable. After a few minutes, I was met by a small child with blond hair and sky-blue eyes. He talked as if he were an adult, but appeared to be only four or five years old. He spread out his hand and showed me what eternity was. At that moment I realized that eternity had no beginning. It never started. The experience is difficult to explain in this short space. I could write a whole book on the nature of eternity. It's enough to say that the realization changed my life.

When I awoke following the procedure, Hetar asked me if I saw anything. I told him about my vision, and he became very interested. He asked me to try to remember every detail. After a few sessions, I asked him why he needed to know about the things I saw during procedures. He said it was because these things were intriguing to him. He said he wanted to know where the visions come from.

I have seen other such visions. Several times I have come across a young man with wavy, golden hair. I know him and we start to talk. He tells me a tale about love and compassion. It is impossible to explain to you how much these things can change one's life, especially when one does not remember them until years later.

Hetar and I often talked about correlation between my experiences with him and the visions I have seen. He seems curious about the fact that these visions are not created or controlled by the ETs, yet they happen anyway, even though the ETs were in total control of the situation on the physical level. A colleague of mine thinks Hetar wants to know because he is amazed by the fact that humans can have these visions while in a time-stop state—something Hetar did not believe humans were capable of without the ETs' help. As of this writing, I do not know.

The ETs like to talk about other realms and other planes of existence. They take us to places where our reality as we know it simply does not exist, and we cope with these things in the best ways we can.

A few days ago, I was on the underground base. I had just finished my work and was talking to a young boy. Hetar was nearby, listening. The boy made a statement, and I replied, "...Well, that's because electricity is invisible. You can see lightning and sparks, but that's just the hot air where the electricity shot through it. Electricity in itself is invisible."

Hetar called me aside, took my hand and said. "I must remind you. Nothing is invisible."

Suddenly I was standing at Hetar's side in an odd environment. It was white with no real features, except some faint colors here and there. In front of me, about three paces away, was a squiggling mass of cobalt-blue lines. They hummed and moved past me from right to left, left to right, all at the same time.

"Everything can be seen from somewhere," Hetar said. "This is electricity. As you are now, it is visible to you." He swung his hand in a motion, as if inviting me to look at the electricity.

I stood there and looked at it for a while longer. It felt strange in the air, and I was uncomfortable.

"Remember, everything is visible from some place," he said. "And everything has a total opposite that complements it completely and totally."

I guess he threw that in for good measure. Maybe he felt that I needed a reminder on that, too.

If you are an experiencer, the more you remember, the more you will be amazed by things and events that could only be described as magical. With ETs, we fly, move through time and space, see things beyond the physical realms, and touch eternity.

As you explore your deeper memories, you will begin to discover the more spiritual side of the experience. Be prepared for it, and don't be afraid. It is a beautiful thing. But be cautious—it can lead you into a confusing maze if you listen to others before you listen to your own heart.

Everyone around you will have an opinion about spirituality—an opinion they will defend with a passion and push at you with endless words. Many people find themselves entrapped into thinking that everyone else must believe what they believe. So they are quick to tell someone who believes differently that he is wrong.

It's sad. After all, no matter what you or anyone else believes, it is a personal and deep part of you—a part of you that should be respected. Far too often, this just is not the case. So, follow your heart—and not your head—when making decisions about anything of a spiritual nature. And remember, religion and spiritually are not the same thing.

Though your spiritual concepts of what life is could have a lot to do with your concept of religion, your religious affiliations may not always represent your total spiritual life. Only your heart can tell you what you really believe. If your heart tells you that what the ETs are showing you is not real, then don't waste time believing it. If someday your heart's view changes, you may find yourself rethinking your position about what you have been taught, which brings me back to the theme of Earth changes.

Sure, things are happening. The Earth is a living planet and is constantly changing. Ask any scientist and he or she can tell you that what we are doing to our world is leading us toward major problems. It does not take a prophet to see that there are going to be some big changes soon. But it does not mean the "end of the world."

Maybe the ETs are conditioning us (their valued subjects) to keep ourselves alive through a nuclear war. After watching what humankind has already done, they have no doubt that we have the ability and nature to do something as crazy as nuclear war.

Many experiencers are told that they will be picked up before things get too bad (so that they will not be harmed) and then returned when the New Order starts.

I know this chapter contains a lot of mixed messages, but it is difficult to talk about this subject in any particular way and still have it apply to all levels of abduction. Experienced Geminis might contend that I have not written enough about the spiritual messages. But then again, you know it already. I don't need to tell you.

If you are a quick in/quick out or a Gemini who is just starting your journey, you may be confused already by what I have written about because you cannot remember experiencing anything like it yet.

Also, it is often difficult for some experiencers to separate what they experience on their own and what the ETs make them live through. So they view things in an all-or-nothing context. But that is not the best way. One must look at every individual piece of the puzzle, study it, and meditate on it before trying to fit it into the whole.

Ultimately, whether or not these Earth changes and social restructuring take place will be ours to find out. The ETs told me that the timeline for their occurrence is before 2004.

People have been predicting the end of the world or some kind of mass destruction and reorganization since time started. So, don't stop closing on your 30-year mortgage or cancel the kids' college funds. Remember, this could all be just another mind game. That is up to you to decide.

No matter what you decide, take heart. Live your life for each day, as you already do. If these changes are truly coming, then you can feel secure in the fact that you are a part of it, and will grow with it, rather than being destroyed by it. If they are not going to happen, you have not lost anything if you don't waste your life living in fear and anxiety. No matter what you decide about this side of the abduction phenomenon, you will grow from it. You cannot let it destroy your life. Never live in fear of what will be. After all, life itself is an uncertainty. We all know that someday our existence on Earth will end—but we need not live in constant fear of our deaths. If we were to do so, we would never live.

Not everyone is exposed to the "spiritual side" of the experience. Perhaps this is because of their level of the abduction experience, or maybe they simply chose not to remember it. A lot of responsibility is connected with the spiritual side. Many are just not ready to commit to that kind of thing yet.

The community of Gemini people is very real—even if it has nothing to do with the nonphysical side. It may be nothing more than the fact that we are all put together at a young age and grow as a family. It may be that we are psychically bonded together by the work of the empaths. It may be that we are a specially trained work force operating as a team in the world beyond—or maybe we are all connected on the deepest soul level, as the ETs tell us we are.

Touch another abductee and you will see what I mean. This is another thing about which you must draw your own conclusions. Often, people will believe the explanation that they feel most comfortable with at that point in their life.

Even though most of what is in this chapter sounds a bit nasty and apocalyptic, there is vast beauty in the spiritual side of your discovery. The beauty inside you is not in me to write about, and the beauty inside me will not satisfy your unique needs. I suggest that you spend some time meditating and thinking about it. Focus on your place in the eternal universe. Contemplate your right to exist in the vastness of time. It will reveal to you a world you know little about—the world of your heart.

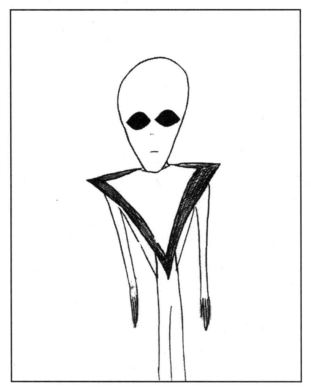

Figure 10. Hetar in uniform.

chapter eleven

Myths and Misconceptions

In this chapter, I will discuss some of the common myths, misconceptions and just plain lies about the aliens. It is important to clear up some of them. Often, when experiencers hear these common misconceptions, they become confused. They can begin to doubt their own validity. It's very important that you never let anyone invalidate you. Never let anyone make you feel as if you are not really experiencing what you know you are.

Since there is more than one kind of ET, one can easily be confused when someone talks about myths regarding ETs. As I explained in chapter one, my experiences deal primarily with the little gray people. I have also shared experiences with the "Nordics" (light-haired, humanoid beings with surreal-colored eyes that have oval pupils). I also have experiences that involve a "Council of Women." I know them as the "Sisters of Time." Other abductees have seen reptilian ETs, or even ETs that look like Bigfoot or Sasquatch.

I cannot recall ever seeing a Bigfoot. Hetar once showed me a picture of an ET that looked like a humanoid/lobster/lizard mix. He told me to be careful of these ETs. I asked why. He said "Because they will eat you." I honestly can't say whether he was teasing me or whether he meant it, but other experiencers have been told the same thing.

The important thing to remember is that each experiencer and the events of his life are unique to him. Even though we are all exposed to similar things, the way each of us perceives events will vary greatly depending on his level of fear or acceptance and his placement in the Gemini community.

Since the majority of the experiencers I know are involved with the little gray people (and since most of the myths and misconceptions I have heard concern them), they are the ETs that I talk about in this chapter unless I say otherwise.

It is easy to see how some of the following misconceptions got started. Others are hard to fathom.

1. ETs cannot talk (with sound) and only communicate telepathically.

Actually, they talk, laugh and cry. Their voices tend to sound nasal, and when they speak English, they pronounce their words with a rather mechanical tone. The closest thing I can find to describe their laugh is the sound of a squirrel chirping, only faster. I cannot describe the sound of their crying. I have heard it only once or twice, a long time ago.

I believe the myth that they are unable talk comes from the fact that when they do talk, their mouths barely move. I'm not suggesting that they can't communicate through telepathy. They can do that and talk, too.

2. The ETs have no lips, and do not open their mouths.

They actually do have a soft rim around their mouths, what we know as lips. Their lips do not show on their faces because they are the same color as their skin and lean into their mouths. They have nasal slits, but no protruding noses, and they have a hard, gum-like jaw in place of teeth. Maybe that is why almost every halfling I have seen has strangely arranged teeth.

This point about lips caused me some personal trouble. I was told by someone who was supposed to know (a well-read non-experiencer) that since ETs have no lips, I must be imagining everything. When I checked the point with other experiencers and a few ETs, I discovered that I had been right.

Even if I had been wrong, I should not have let anyone else's words bother me so badly. Everyone makes mistakes, but we experiencers tend to be harder on ourselves than others. This is because we are fighting not only with the people around us for validity, but with ourselves as well. It is difficult for experiencers to learn to trust their inner voices.

3. The ETs have cold, clammy skin.

ETs have soft, smooth, warm skin. They are not cold, clammy or snake-like, despite what some non-experiencers say.

This misconception probably comes from the cold tone of their skin.

4. All ETs who are called greys are gray.

Though I have seen mostly little people with an ashen pallor, I have also seen ETs who have skin with a pale blue tone in the company of the gray ones. Many experiencers I know have also seen ETs with pale white, yellow and even golden skin. I have actually heard of experiencers who have seen bright purple or red skin.

This color variation is probably from a combination of things. Not only could the perceptions of the experiencer having the encounter affect the color of ETs they see, but the ETs themselves more than likely have pigment variations, as our own human race does. Another aspect that can contribute to color variation is the lighting of the environment. If an event takes place in a room that is brightly lit with red or purple light, the ETs' neutral-colored bodies may reflect that light, giving them the appearance of being the color of the room light around them, in much the same way a white shirt will glow red in the red light of a photographer's darkroom.

Some people believe that ETs of different colors are different races of aliens with different purposes for being here. You may even hear people say, "The gray ones are bad, but the gold ones are good," or vice versa. Judging from my experience and from talking to other abductees, I believe that there is no major notable difference between the messages and behavior of greys of different skin tones.

Still, it is important to know that these differences in color do exist. If your memories deal primarily with ETs who are not basically gray, it does not mean that your memories are wrong or not real. It simply means that ETs you know appear to be a different color from the ETs someone else knows—nothing more.

5. The ETs have long tentacles, like fingers covered with suction cups, similar to those found on an octopus.

Although many people remember seeing ETs using long, tube-like tools that appear to have suction devices on them, the ETs' actual hands are long and thin with four fingers. When their hands are lying open on a flat surface, they appear wide, with a small amount of webbing at the base of each finger. When they are hanging by their sides, they are slender and long, giving the ETs' already proportionally long arms an even longer appearance.

This misconception of what the ETs' hands look like may have started because of confusion between the instruments they use and their hands.

Although it is common knowledge among abductees that the ETs have only four fingers, some debunkers have pointed out that most cartoon characters have only four fingers. They may be trying to imply that we are fantasizing our abductions because we created our ETs with cartoon attributes. This is totally ridiculous. The fact that some cartoon characters have four fingers does not mean that any being with four fingers is a cartoon. Don't let these types of feeble arguments bother you.

6. ETs eyes are deep black. They have no pupils.

The ETs' eyes are very sensitive to light. Their living quarters are dimly lit. When they are in a situation where more light is required, or when they may be subject to having a light shone at them by surprise, they wear the black lenses that have turned into their trademark.

When I was a child, I asked Hetar why he didn't just get sunglasses. Then I realized that it would be hard to wear glasses with barely any protruding nose and ears.

7. You can do things or carry objects with you to keep ETs away.

A common misconception is that sleeping with the TV or radio on will keep ETs away. Some people even believe that spreading salt on one's windowsills, placing crystals around one's bed or wearing amethyst necklaces will deter them. These ideas are nothing more than wishful thinking, probably first proposed by someone going through pickup anxiety.

I was even told by one of my experiencer colleagues that humming loudly would cause them to leave me alone or bring me right back home. She said she was told that the vibrations of the humming bothers them. (What is this, the alien version of Super Bug-Away?)

Despite my last remark, I really do try to keep my mind open to everyone's suggestions. So I decided to try it the last time I was picked up.

I was in a room with Hetar and four other greys. I remembered what my friend said and started to hum, very loudly in the exact tone she taught me. Nothing happened.

I kept it up. After a few minutes or so, Hetar came to me and asked, "Are you all right?"

I didn't answer. I just kept on humming.

"Are you in pain? Do you need something from me?" he asked.

When I failed to answer a second time, they just ignored me and continued with their work. I was not brought home–even when I changed the tone of the hum (in case I had it wrong). So it was useless— a simple waste of time. It didn't do much for my voice either.

I asked my Gemini friend Jon to try it. He had no luck either. He said he felt ridiculous. All either of us proved was that, humming constantly for a half hour or more, will cause one to wake up with a sore, dry throat.

Maybe this appeared to work for someone at one time. So, I can only presume that the abductee's humming was bothersome to the greys working on him, so they knocked the abductee out for the rest of the procedures. When the person woke up at home, his last memory was of humming. So he put the two together and figured that since he remembered nothing after he started to hum, the humming caused the greys to bring him directly home. It seems to be just another case of perception to me.

I suppose that the explanation works, subjectively. But if you think it will get you home on demand, good luck to you. It didn't work for me or Jon, and we both felt very foolish afterward.

8. All people who are abducted will see their rooms fill with blue light.

Though waking up to a room of pale blue light before an abduction event is very common, it is not a hard and fast rule. Some experiencers have no memories of ever waking up to blue light. Others remember waking up to white light, yellow light, even orange light. Many people wake up to a buzzing sound in one or both ears. Some remember no prelude to an abduction event at all. Again, perception is the key here. Although many experiencers have the ability to feel when aliens are nearby, most will be sound asleep when the ETs contact them. So, even if the room is filled with blue or white light, the experiencer may not be awake enough to be aware of it.

9. Only bad or evil people are abducted by ETs.

Never let anyone tell you that you are an abduction experiencer because you did something bad. Twice I have heard people say such things. On both occasions I was with a group of non-experiencers talking about the abduction experience in a very spontaneous fashion. None of the others in the group knew that I was an abductee. They said things like, "You ever notice how aliens only abduct people out in the woods, polishing off their fourth case of beer?" or "People who are abducted are all some kind of freaks, and God has forsaken them." Once I even heard someone say on national TV that abduction experiencers are all members of an evil alien worshiping cult run by Satan!

You know that statements like these are born out of ignorance; don't let them get to you.

10. The ETs are little robot-like creatures who will not talk to you.

Another myth about the greys is that they will not talk to experiencers. They just silently do their job like little robots.

It is true that if an abductee is screaming frantically they may not pay attention to her. But if she handles herself reasonably, they will take the time to talk to her. But she must be prepared to hear the truth. If she finds the courage to ask, "What are you going to do to me?" she should be ready to hear what they plan to do. They will tell her, no matter how upsetting the answer.

I will never forget how I felt when once I asked what they were going to do to me. "We are going to take your lungs out. Does that scare you?" was the answer. Someone else I know was shocked to see an ET holding a very long needle. He said it resembled a prop from a Three Stooges movie. When he asked what they were intending to do with it, he was told they were going to put it into his side. Then, much to his horror, they did.

11. Abductees have no control over when and where these things happen.

Another misconception is that the experiencer has no control over when his or her abduction occurs. Actually, we do have a limited control. For instance, if an abductee is cooking supper and suddenly feels an incredibly strong urge to go out and take a walk in the woods behind her house, she can choose to fight it.

Stopping them from coming to get you in the middle of the night is a different matter. If you manage to open a dialogue with them, you might be able to gain enough respect from them to persuade them not to bother you on a particular night, if you ask them not to.

Does this really work? I can only say that it appears to, if it is not used too often. Try it.

12. The ETs are angels sent here by God or demons.

This myth gave me quite a bit of trouble. In my first support environment, I was surrounded by experiencers who believed the ETs were angels sent from heaven. I never could accept that fully. After all, what would an angel need a spaceship for?

The gray ETs are enlightened beings who are further along the evolutionary and spiritual scale than we are, but they are *not* angels. Their enlightenment, like all growth, came at a great cost and after plenty of mistakes. After all, wisdom is a child born of a hard labor.

Despite their wisdom and knowledge, they are beings more like you and me than they are different from us. Along with their great advances, they still have what we like to call "human" flaws. Angels are supposed to be perfect.

A person I looked to for guidance kept telling me that I was wrong to doubt her. I will call her Lillian. She said that the ETs were angels, and she truly believed this. Though I respected her belief, I found this extremely confusing because I simply could not bring myself to see it that way. My heart did not feel it.

Finally, I resolved to ask Hetar if he was an angel. I felt I really needed to know. So, the next time I saw him, I told him I had to talk to him. He and I found a quiet place in the base and we sat down to talk. I got up my nerve and asked him. "Hetar, are you an angel?"

He cocked his head in that way they often do, and chuckled. "No, I'm not," he said very directly.

"But Lillian said you are," I said.

"At Lillian's stage of growth, she would perceive me as an angel. I expect more from you," he replied.

They are very special people, but they are not angels. I suppose it is not harmful to perceive them that way if you wish, but you may find yourself confused when you remember them doing something totally un-angelic out of "human" imperfections.

Neither are the ETs demons. I'm not proposing that angels and demons don't exist—only that you will not see them flying a spaceship, time ship, ship of light or anything else you choose to call the alien craft.

13. Hypnosis makes abduction events stop.

Another myth is that once one undergoes hypnosis, the abductions stop.

If the ETs are aware that an abductee is seeing a hypnotherapist, they might bury future experiences deeper in her subconscious mind, so that she will not remember too quickly. Or, in some cases, abductees may be so involved in remembering details of events that surface under hypnosis that they fail to remember current events.

There are many other, less common myths and misconceptions. You may encounter some on your own personal journey that I am not aware of.

No matter what you hear or read, don't let anything destroy your confidence in yourself.

Remember the concept of perception. If you and someone you know experience the same event, the ways each of you perceives the event will have a lot to do with the way you remember it, and what you learn from it.

Reality is subjective. This means, in simple terms, what is perceived as real to you *is* real to you.

Eventually, as you grow, you will begin to let go of the fear and see things more clearly. Remember Lillian. She is not ready to see the ETs as anything less than perfect, angelic beings because in this stage of her growth, she cannot accept that her life is so controlled by "another life form." It is much more comforting to think that she is being taken by angels than by aliens. Isn't it?

14. Alien abduction is always a fearful and traumatic experience.

This may seem true to many abductees when they first start exploring their experiences, but it is simply not so. Although just about all of us will encounter fear when we first start to explore our events, if allowed to confront our fears and grow past them, we will find that our experiences are on the whole positive and enlightening. As I mentioned before, most of the time our fears come from how we interpret the hazy incomplete memories we have of procedures and reaction tests. As we explore deeper into these experiences and the details begin to fill in, we often find that they were not as horrible as we first recalled. This is especially true for abductees who are members of the Gemini community. Since passionate emotions are easier to remember, often events that cause us feelings of fear or confusion will hamper us from feelings of community and peace we are used to when we interact with our ET and Gemini brothers and sisters.

It is easy to see how this myth got started. After all, fear is a common human response to things we don't understand. It is a frustrating myth to dispel, particularly because the media in general makes a point to slant their UFO/ET related stories to ones of fear and panic. There are even several researchers who would want abductees to believe this myth to be true. They say that experiencers who are not afraid of what is happening to them are hiding from the truth. But this is in itself a myth. When abductees face their fears and work through them, they find that the ET encounter experience is one of growth and wonder. Most experiencers who have broken through the fear barrier actually look forward to contact with the ETs and feel like these little gray people are part of their extended family.

I know that if you are living through the fear right now, this myth feels like fact, but someday you will know it is just a myth. I have no doubt that the deeper you explore into your personal journey of discovery, the less fear you will have. Again, growth is the key.

So, that's it for major myths. Everything I told you is true. These are not just theories or ideas of mine. These are things I know after discussing abductions with Hetar, after talking with many other experiencers, and after years of firsthand encounters.

chapter twelve

Taking Control

I hope that by now you are feeling a little more clear on what has been happening to you. So now it's time to talk about taking control of the situation and empowering yourself. It is important that you be in charge of your life and happy with the role you play in the experience.

Conquering Pickup Anxiety

To start with, you have to get over pickup anxiety. To do this, you should practice a few simple techniques:

1. Visualization to control startle reflex

Begin by visualizing yourself encountering the ETs in your home. Start with the most common place, your bedroom. Lie down on your bed and picture yourself waking up to find them standing at the foot of your bed. Concentrate on making an effort not to be startled or jump.

Close your eyes and picture them standing there, then open your eyes quickly. You may feel tense and be a little frightened to open your eyes, but you have to do it. Say to yourself, "I know they are there. I will not startle. I will stay calm."

Practice this several times each night and each time you feel uneasy. Keep practicing until you feel sure you can control your startle reflex.

When the time comes that you are picked up by the ETs, do your best not to be startled, just as you did in practice. If you succeed, take the next step forward.

2. Resolve to talk to the ETs

Once you have handled your startle reflex, the next step is to point out to the ETs the fact that you did not startle. Tell them that you will make an effort not to startle in the future, and, therefore, it is not necessary for them to stun you. If you are physically unable to talk, simply think the words to them. They will hear you. Try not to think negative, hurtful things in their presence, as they can hear you, and this will set you back.

3. Passing the test

If you keep it up (not startling and attempting to talk to them), soon they will test you. They might stand out of your reach and wake you. They might wake you with the urge to enter another room, where an ET waits to observe your reaction. If you are able to avoid panic, you have taken a major step forward. You have gained their trust.

This is how they tested me: At about 5:00 A.M., I got up to nurse my child. After the baby fell asleep, I returned him to his room. I saw an ET standing by the window. I didn't panic. I just said "Hello, what are you doing here?" I was surprised to see him so close to daylight. I was even more surprised that all my practicing held up and I didn't panic. I stood there, staring at him, until he seemed to disappear into the room's curtains. (See Figure 11.)

When I returned to my bed, my sheets were rolled in a ball on my pillow and my comforter was completely upside down with my husband sound asleep on top of it all. I started to laugh. Their little joke let me know I did fine.

4. Go by yourself (if given the opportunity).

As you are picked up time and time again without becoming startled, they may even allow you to go by yourself.

You may find yourself waking gently to the blue light. Don't panic or become startled; just walk into the light as a volunteer. From that point on, pickup anxiety is a thing of the past. You will never have another traumatic pickup event.

Often I am awakened by a gentle stroking on my hair or face. When I open my eyes, I am greeted with gentle words of encouragement and welcome. I get up and walk into the light by myself.

When you reach this stage in your relationship with the ETs, you can, on occasion, tell them, "Not tonight, please." If you don't do it too often, and if they don't need you for something extremely important, they will respect your choice.

Figure 11. Michelle remains calm as she meets a grey in her baby's room.

By keeping your fear response in check, you force them to realize that you are intelligent enough to control your terror. You are too smart to give in to animal reaction. You have now gained their respect.

As their respect grows, so will your position in their structure. As they see that you are more than just a scared animal, they will give you more responsibilities. And the better you do with the new responsibilities, the more they will trust you.

If you are now a quick in/quick out, you will soon be a working part of the Gemini community, and you will have much more control over the things that happen around you. You may even begin to attend classes or lectures held by the ETs.

It seems that the more responsibility you have in the Gemini community, the less medical work is done on you—although I do know several people who still participate occasionally in the breeding program by choice, because they feel it is important.

Another good way to empower yourself is to keep a good attitude. After all, this is your life and you have to make of it what you can. The ETs believe you contracted to do this before you were born. So they expect you to live up to your commitment without hesitation. If you don't feel you have contracted to do this, tell them so. Don't waste your time and breath asking questions like, "Why me?"

Be forward with them and say, "I don't want to do this anymore," if that's truly what you feel. But before you do, take the time to explore every aspect of your experiences.

Although the ETs are not likely to honor your wish to be left alone (remember that they have an agenda and you are part of it), there is always the possibility it may happen. If it does, you may find you don't want your contact to end after all.

Face your fears and anxieties. Meditate and reflect on who you are (or more importantly, on *why* you are).

Meditation

Often when people hear the word "meditation," they think of a guru in a temple atop a mountain, chanting "ohm." Meditation isn't so difficult.

The easiest way I know to meditate is very simple. Find yourself a quiet place where you feel comfortable. Unplug your phone (or turn on your answering machine). Sit or lie down. Clear your mind of any strong thoughts or worries by focusing on an object or a sound in your room, or by closing your eyes and looking at the back of your eyelids.

Take a few deep "cleansing" breaths, then start to breathe in a regular, even pattern. With each breath, imagine that you are inhaling beautiful, relaxing colors and wonderfully fresh air. When you exhale, imagine that you are releasing all the worry and pain from your soul as dark colors. As you breathe out the dark air, you inhale bright colorful "good" air to replace it.

Allow the colors to fill you to the very corners of your being. You will probably see oranges and greens at first, but as the meditation goes on—or as you do it more—you may soon start to see violets and fuchsias. The ETs teach us that purples are the colors of balance. Since balance is what you are striving for in general, strive for purple.

As you relax into your meditation, you can do one of several things:

1. Allow the colors to come to you as you breathe them in, and see if they develop into anything. (Sometimes they may develop into pictures of events or people.)
2. Picture yourself sitting where you are, on the Earth, and "zoom" out away from yourself until you see how small you really are in eternity. This can be incredibly awe-inspiring. Just think of how small we all are in the eternal universe, yet we all have a right and a reason to exist.
3. Think of a question or problem and seek out a solution.
4. Talk to the universe. Ask it to teach you.
5. Concentrate on someone else and direct the beautiful colors you are seeing toward them, to help them.
6. Think about an event. Let the details come to you.
7. Locate your center. Contemplate your center and then strive to achieve that center.

This last exercise is by far the most important. You should make a habit of trying to do this on a regular basis.

What is center? Center is that part of you that keeps all parts of you balanced and all parts of your life in focus.

What is *your* center? I wish I could tell you, but only you can go through the door of your mind, get inside and find that answer. You have to look into yourself before you can bring out every answer you need. The hardest thing you will be asked to do is grow. But grow you must. So you might as well make the best of it.

You are a traveler on an incredible journey. See yourself that way.

So, in summing up, I urge you to:
1. Keep a written record of your experiences and how you feel about them.
2. Practice not startling or panicking.
3. Resolve to talk to the ETs.
4. Try to find other experiencers who understand what you are feeling—people with whom you

can talk about your experiences.

5. Keep a positive attitude. No matter how down you feel, don't allow yourself to live like a victim anymore.
6. Don't just talk, but listen to your support network.
7. Try to focus on your strengths and not your fears.
8. Meditate often, always being sure to visualize bright, warm colors in and around you, and always trying to find your center.
9. Love every part of the living universe. They are us and we are them.
10. Strive to grow and understand the total of your experiences.

For whatever reason—or perhaps for no reason at all—you were chosen for this unusual role in life. You have come a long way, and you still have a long way to go to discover who you really are. Never forget that you are not a "lab rat," and don't let anyone tell you that you are.

You are a member of the Secret Community. You are living in blue light. What is happening to you *is* real. It is *not* a dream. It is not a lunatic's delusion.

It is part of what you are.

Remember, you are a very special person living in a time of wonder. May light and love follow you.

For Support People

Although this book was written for you, the alien abduction experiencer, this appendix is also for your nonexperiencer support person (or persons, if you are lucky enough to have more than one). Sometimes it's easy to forget them in the rush of new emotions around us. Often, the support person stands around in total confusion, feeling helpless, while we run around in our fury to find out as much about ourselves as we can in as short a time as possible. When this happens, the support person can become more invisible than the "unseen" aliens.

The non-abductee support people are the unsung heroes of this grand game of discovery. After all, you expect them to accept something on faith that you had a hard time accepting with proof. And they do, because they love you. When you, the experiencer, read this chapter, keep in mind that these feelings are going through your support person every day.

Ask them to read this book, so that they can understand some of what is happening to you. If they choose not to, ask them at least to read this appendix. To write it, I relied heavily on the experiences and feelings of the special support people in my life and in the lives of other abductees. (While reading this, remember that it all applies to both male and female abductees and support people, regardless of which personal pronoun I use in this text.)

As a support person of an abduction experiencer, your life is one day of confusion after another. Your life has been completely reconstructed in a very unfamiliar way. It is probably very hard for you to accept what your loved one tells you is happening to them.

If you did not believe in UFOs or aliens before all of this came up to the surface, it has been twice as difficult for you. After all, you are not only being asked to believe in something you don't believe in, you are also expected to believe that these ETs are visiting your loved one on a regular basis.

Often, even if you believe in UFOs and abductions, it is very difficult to come to terms with the fact that it's happening to someone around you. This is especially hard if the abductee is a child, spouse or someone else you feel very protective of.

Doubt

One of the first feelings you may experience is doubt. Many support people try to explain what the abductee is telling them in more familiar ways. One woman I know would listen to her experiencer husband talk about what he remembered, then tell him he was having bad dreams from watching too much TV at night. Another person I know had a husband who was convinced she was having a mental breakdown and threatened to have her committed.

One of the most upsetting things to a support person—and often to the experiencer who is in denial as well—is confirmation, through hypnosis or through scars and common descriptions, that an abduction memory is real.

I know many support people who have gone through periods during which they wished the abductee was actually "crazy." Crazy was something they could understand; abducted by aliens was not. Besides, you can get some treatment to cure insanity. You cannot cure experiencers; they aren't sick.

Depression

The next thing that usually happens after you discover that the events are real is a sense of depression. This often happens because you are told that you are powerless to change your situation. This is not entirely true, but many "experts" in the infant science of abduction studies think it is. Sometimes support people jump past this stage and go directly into anger. They may or may not become depressed later.

Depression can result from the seemingly hopeless messages abductees remember after delving deeply into their experiences. My husband was completely devastated by what I remembered under my first hypnosis session. After it was over, the doctor asked him, "How does what she said make you feel?"

My husband said, "How is it supposed to make me feel? I mean what's the point of buying Christmas presents for the kids? Why go to work tomorrow?" He spent a long time after that night feeling totally depressed with no hope for the future. He said he felt as if he were walking in a bad dream. He had no will to live. If it had not been for our children, he said, he would have been tempted to "let it all go." Luckily, with time, he recovered from these feelings.

As the abductee begins to talk about the visions she has been shown by the ETs, you may become confused by how little these pictures of "gloom and doom" appear to affect the experiencer. Actually, she is affected very deeply, but the experience and the idea behind it are not as new to her as they are to you. They are just new to her conscious memory.

Some support people are shocked by the way some abductees choose to handle the horror of these remembered visions. Some experiencers go through the "Everyone-is-going-to-die-and-it-will-be-wonderful" mindset, which is shocking to anybody. You must understand that this is the way they handle the incomplete messages they are remembering.

If your relationship with the experiencer is weak, you may find that the stress surrounding this is too much to handle, and you may find yourself looking for a way out of the relationship. Even if your relationship is strong, you may find yourself contemplating running away. This is very normal and understandable, but don't let it happen. The strain may seem like it will never end. Still, it does…slowly. Most couples who ride it out together have become stronger because of the experiences.

In order to understand and cope with what is going on around you, you must understand what the abductee is feeling. The first thing to point out is that abductees may seem sure in themselves and their belief of what is happening to them, but they often go through times when they doubt themselves or simply wish they were "nuts" rather than abductees. During these times of doubt, they may stop talking about their experiences. They may even stop attending support-group meetings or seeing friends who are also experiencers in order to think things over without outside influences, without people telling them what to believe. Sometimes they may think that if they stop talking about it, it will go away.

Many times, support people interpret these quiet times as "It's all over." They think everything has stopped and the abductees are not being bothered by the ETs anymore. In fact, these things will never stop. They have been happening throughout the experiencers' lives, and will continue until they die. (In a few cases, people who were not deeply involved with the ETs reportedly lost their ability to produce eggs or sperm, and were left alone for the rest of their lives. But this is not always the case, so please don't start planning to have your husband castrated or your wife's ovaries removed to stop abductions.)

If you let these quiet times create a false sense of safety, you may be shaken when the abductee starts everything all over again. You may be surprised to know how many support people fall into this pattern, time and time again. Each time, they are equally upset and confused by the sudden change.

I also want to warn you not to fall into the cycles of fear. Sometimes an experiencer becomes so afraid of what is happening to her—or even of what is happening to you, or of the way you react when she talks about her abductions—that she tells you it's over, and nothing is happening anymore, in order to protect you from it. You may believe her. If you do, you are only asking for a bigger problem in the future. She can only keep up the charade for so long before either telling you the truth (and hurting your relationship and trust), or confiding in someone else. Either way, you lose.

So if the experiencer tells you something like, "They are never coming back. I'm sure of it," just say something like, "Let's just take it one day at a time. They still may come back."

Don't tell her, "Yes, they'll be back. Don't lie to me." This will only put her on the defensive. You have to keep in mind that the abductee may be trying to protect you, not deceive you.

Anger

Before long, most support people become angry. It's very hard not to. They have no control over the situation, yet someone is depending on them to stay strong and be understanding through it all.

You must try to control your anger. Experiencers are very sensitive to other peoples' emotions. They tend to absorb them. All experiencers have a heightened sixth sense, and quite a few of them are trained empaths. They may not even be aware of these things in their conscious state, yet it will still affect their lives. Because of this, they cannot help but feel your anger, even if you don't express it.

You may be very angry at the ETs for what is happening and not at the abductee, but unless you talk to the abductee about what's going on in your head, she will probably believe the anger is directed at her.

One of the hardest things for her to do is watch the pain her experiences are putting you through. For this reason, she may feel like you have a right to be angry at her. So, when she senses anger, she could easily assume it is directed at her. Be reassuring and spend at least a little time every day or so talking about your feelings with the experiencer.

Anger usually comes from a feeling of helplessness. Some support people will try anything to end the helpless feelings. It is not unusual for the spouse of an abductee to sleep with a weapon beside his bed to stop the ETs. Please don't do this. It is useless in defending yourself from ETs, but it could easily hurt someone you love. The ETs will paralyze you before they enter your home. They may even knock you out completely. Either way, the weapon is useless. If you can pick up that gun and fire it at the small figure standing at the foot of your bed, you may shoot one of your children.

A much better "weapon" to have at your bedside (if you still think you should have one) is a flashlight. Then, when you see that figure in your room, you can beam the light at the figure. You may startle your child (or your cat), but that is infinitely better than putting a bullet through her. And you will feel much safer if you can see what is going on than if you must guess what shadows are. And if on the odd chance it happens that the figure is an ET, the beam of bright light flashed at his sensitive eyes may deter him.

Getting over the fear of being helpless is one of the toughest things you must do as a support person. You have to sit there and try to understand what the experiencer is going through. You will be able to see some things much more clearly and objectively than the abductee can. You may find yourself feeling that she is looking for trouble. During her search for understanding, she may look in very unusual places and meet the most bizarre people.

I think this happens because the UFO experience is almost always lumped together with other strange (and sometimes questionable) phenomena, such as Bigfoot, the lost city of Atlantis, etc. And, unfortunately, there are few places that an abductee can go to find books and other material about the experience. Most of these places are New Age centers and bookstores.

Can you image how confusing it can be for the newly aware abductee who walks into a New Age store full of books that claim to explain everything anyone would ever need to know about the alien experience, reads a few books, and discovers that they are written by people who know little about it after all?

Some of these books are good sources of information for the general public, but there is a definite flood of misinformation being spread out there. Scientists and doctors who research the phenomenon have written some reasonably accurate books, but they are directed toward non-experiencers, and may leave an abductee feeling very lost.

I do not intend to imply that New Age book stores are bad places. Most are wonderful places staffed by people who really care about what they are selling to the public. Many experiencers can be lost in the wonder of the New Age movement and confuse the movement with their mission to discover themselves. The two can often appear very similar. If this happens, they can go off on some strange tangent and find themselves totally lost.

These can be the most frustrating times of all for the support people. Just as you are becoming accustomed to the idea that alien craft are visiting your home, the experiencer comes running in the door, talking excitedly about the nature of eternity or the order of the universe. These things are very important, but I'm sure you couldn't care less. After all, who cares if eternity has no beginning or end and all the theology behind it? You have all the everyday stresses from life. And you have to keep convincing the experiencer that you are not upset by the things she tells you, even though those things are tearing your insides out. How could you worry about the meaning of crop circles when you have to make your mortgage payment next Monday? All of a sudden, you and the experiencer are living in two completely different worlds.

You must have a hard time coping with the breakneck speed at which most experiencers run forward into any situation that they feel could answer some of their questions. If your loved one starts to rush into a situation that you feel uncomfortable with, talk to her about it. Never tell her, "No, you can't do that." That will only promote a feeling of need, and the need will encourage the feeling of panic some abduct- ees experience.

Many abductees feel as if they have an inner clock ticking away in- side them. They feel as if they are running out of time, and must hurry to discover themselves. If you notice your loved one running headlong into things (leaping before she looks), talk to her. Encourage her to wait a few extra days. If the situation is right for her, then it will still be right tomorrow. If it's wrong, perhaps a good night's sleep or two will make that clear. If not, don't stop her. Instead of arguing, offer to go with her to check it out. Be open-minded—but keep your eyes and ears open.

I have seen experiencers get hurt because they wanted so desper- ately to have a place to go for answers that they closed their eyes to bad situations. I know one young girl who believed she was in a support group for abductees, but soon found out she was involved in a bizarre alien-worship cult. (There is a difference between an experiencer seeing the ETs as angels and worshipping them as gods.)

On the other hand, I have seen abductees hurt because their sup- port people were so afraid of what was going on around them that they made it hard for the experiencer to get any help at all. If you find your- self telling the experiencer that an idea or group she comes across is bad or wrong, you should take a good look at your inner motives. Are you really protecting the abductee or yourself?

You may also find yourself upset or confused by the fact that, somewhere inside you, you are thinking, "Better her than me." That's another normal reaction. As a matter of fact, you may find that if your loved one tells you she saw you on the ship with the ETs, you will say something like, "That's impossible! I'm not the abductee here—you are." (Actually, if anyone is getting the raw end of the deal, it *is* you. You are receiving all the stress and reaping few of the rewards.)

Even though it may seem hard to believe, things will settle down and start to make sense. You might feel a bit insecure as you see the ex- periencer growing and making new relationships. Every one of us has a need to be loved, and it's scary to watch someone we love changing in front of our eyes. When these things happen, support people start to wonder if their abductees will "outgrow" them. But don't be afraid. Love is a wonderful force. Besides, you, too, are growing through this experience (although you may not see it that way).

A few words of warning:

1. On support groups

If you do plan to attend support groups with the experiencer, take them lightly. There are so few groups that the people in any given group are often in various stages of development and understanding. The group environment can be baffling to the nonexperiencer who cannot identify with anyone else in the group. Some groups offer a separate room, where the support people can go to talk to each other if the abductee group gets too heavy. Some support people even hold meetings of their own. You don't have to attend any of these functions if they upset you or bore you. My husband attends very few. He simply dislikes talking about his feelings in public. I respect his choice and don't force him.

2. On hypnosis

If the experiencer you support is going to undergo hypnotic regression, think carefully about whether you want to be there or not. Hypnosis is not like what you see in the movies. Abductees under hypnosis often have violent physical reactions. They can scream and convulse as they remember pain and terror. It can be really hard to watch someone you love relive these experiences.

Since the abduction experience can often be of a sexual nature, some experiencers will not talk about it, even under hypnosis, if their spouses are present, because they don't want to hurt them. So you have a lot to think about. But if you feel you can do it and the abductee wants you there, then you should attend the hypnosis session.

3. Don't forget to take time for yourself.

Everyone has to release his stress somehow. Find a way you like, and do it. Don't ignore yourself, no matter how much is going on with the experiencer. Remember, you cannot help her if you fail to help yourself.

If the things the abductee tells you overwhelm you, don't be afraid to tell her so, and ask her to slow down. It is better to take it slow than to try to go beyond your limits and lose the ability to take it at all.

Glossary of Terms

Be-prepared reaction—A common side effect of reaction test, characterized by an abductee's feeling that something of global proportions may happen at any moment, and he must be ready for it. This may take many forms, ranging from saving water in a basement, to knowing where all the exits are in a building in case "it" happens. This reaction is often a subconscious habit. (See on page 69.)

Chosen-one reaction—A common way of coping with abduction events. By believing that they are better than the rest of the people around them (and therefore were "chosen" by the ETs), abductees can avoid facing many of the harsher issues concerning the abduction event. Most abductees go though this reaction to at least some degree during their lives. (See on page 10.)

Controller—A working part of the Gemini community. Controllers are responsible for directing and regulating other abductees during many events. (See on page 12.)

Cycles—The emotional turnarounds abductees experience when discovering what is happening to them. A typical cycle can start with fear, continue with terror, then fade to uneasiness and finally, calm. After time, calm gives way to tension, then fear, as the cycle starts again. (See on page 21.)

Empath—Gemini workers who are trained to use their minds' abilities to calm, control and heal others. (See on page 13.)

Experiencer—The name chosen by many abductees because they feel the term "abductee" is not appropriate (since they do not feel truly abducted). In this guide, the terms "experiencer" and "abductee" are interchangeable, with no special meaning given to either.

Gemini abductee—A person who experiences more than just "medical" abductions. The Gemini abductee is involved in the community of experiencers created by the ETs. (See on page 6.)

Gray ET—Small, thin beings with gray or ash-white skin color and large, almond-shaped eyes. Most are not much taller than three feet or so; others are notably taller and somewhat thinner. "Greys" are the primary beings most people remember. They are also the principal ETs I discuss in this guide.

Halfling—A hybrid being, part human and part ET.

Hetar—A taller gray ET who I call my mentor. Some abductees call beings like him the "head doctor" or the "leader." He is the being who urged me to write this guide.

New World Order—A name for what the world will be like after the global changes abductees are often told about will occur. (See on page 75.)

Nonlinear time—The concept that time is not moving only in a straight, chronological path forward, but also in all directions and through all realities concurrently. (See on page 66.)

Nordic ET—This type of being is usually seen as a tall, well proportioned human with light hair and unusual colored eyes. They are often seen in the company of greys.

One-time abductee—A person who was picked up by ETs for a specific reason and never bothered again. (See on page 5.)

Phasing—The ability to make one object pass through another.

Pickup anxiety—Tension and fear experienced by abductees concerning the actual moment of abduction. Typical effects of pickup anxiety include fear of the dark or even fear of opening a door at night (because an ET may be waiting behind it). (See on page 44.)

Quick in/quick out abductee—This level of abductee is a regular visitor with the ETs, but the purpose of their abduction is primarily of a medical nature. Quick in/quick out abductees are usually unable to move independently, and are often "processed" through the abduction event in an efficient, assembly-line fashion. (See on page 6.)

Reptilian ET—This form of ET is usually associated with painful, terrifying abduction events. They are, to my knowledge, never seen working with the greys, although the two types are aware of each other. If you are experiencing abduction events with these ETs as well as with the greys or Nordics, talk to the greys or Nordics. I believe they can make the Reptilians stop.

Support Resources

Academy of Certified Close Encounter Therapists (ACCET)
    2826 O St., Ste. 3
    Sacramento, CA 95816
    (for therapist referral)

Connecting Link (magazine)
    9392 Whitneyville Rd. SE
    Alto, MI 49302-9694

Contact Forum (newsletter)
    P. O. Box 726
    Newberg, OR 97132
    800-366-0264
    bluewaterp@aol.com

Institute for the Study of Contact with Non-Human Intelligence (ISCNI)
    3463 State St. #440
    Santa Barbara, CA 93105
    805-563-8500
    ISCNI@aol.com

Michelle LaVigne
    P. O. Box 1862
    Merrimack, NH 03054-1862
    MICKKEE@aol.com

Mutual UFO Network (MUFON)
    103 Oldtowne Rd.
    Seguin, TX 78155-4099
    210-379-9216

OPUS (Organization for Paranormal Understanding and Support)
    Kathy Hennesy
    P. O. Box 273273
    Concord, CA 94527
    510-689-2666

Program for Extraordinary Experience Research (PEER)
    1493 Cambridge St.
    Cambridge, MA 02139
    617-497-2667

The UFO Library (magazine)
    11684 Ventura Blvd., Ste. 708
    Studio City, CA 91604
    714-995-6007

UFO Magazine
    P. O. Box 1053
    Sunland, CA 91041
    818-951-1250

appendix four

Essential Reading

Boylan, Richard J. *Close Extraterrestrial Encounters: Positive Experiences with Mysterious Visitors.* Newberg, OR: Wild Flower Press, 1993. (See related material on page 91.)

Bryant, Alice and Linda Seebach. *Healing Shattered Reality: Understanding Contactee Trauma.* Newberg, OR: Wild Flower Press, 1991.

Davenport, Marc. *Visitors From Time: The Secret of the UFOs.* Murfreesboro, TN: Greenleaf Publications, 1994. (See related material on page 65.)

Fowler, Raymond E. *The Watchers: The Secret Design Behind UFO Abduction.* New York: Bantam Books, 1990.

Fowler, Raymond E. *The Watchers II: Exploring UFOs and the Near-Death Experience.* Newberg, OR: Wild Flower Press, 1995.(See related material on page 77.)

Jacobs, David M. *Secret Life: Firsthand Documented Accounts of UFO Abductions.* New York: Fireside, 1992.

Kannenberg, Ida. *UFOs and the Psychic Factor: How to Understand Encounters with UFOs and ETs.* Newberg, OR: Wild Flower Press, 1992. (See related material on page 96.)

Lindemann, Michael, ed. *UFOs and the Alien Presence: Six Viewpoints.* Newberg, OR: Wild Flower Press reprint, 1995.

Mack, John E. *Abduction: Human Encounters with Aliens.* New York: Scribners, 1994.

Pritchard, Andrea, David E. Pritchard, John E. Mack, Pam Kasey, Claudia Yapp, eds. *Alien Discussions: Proceedings of the Abduction Study Conference.* Cambridge, MA: North Cambridge Press, 1994.